Succeeding at
Jewish Education

Succeeding at Jewish Education

HOW ONE SYNAGOGUE MADE IT WORK

by Joseph Reimer

5/18

Foreword

by Jonathan Woocher

The Jewish Publication Society
Philadelphia and Jerusalem

Manufactured in the United States of America

Library of Congress Cataloging-in-Publication Data
Reimer, Joseph
    Succeeding at Jewish education : how one synagogue make it work /
    by Joseph Reimer.
        p.   cm.
Includes bibliographical references.
ISBN 0–8276–0623–0
1. Jewish religious education—United States.   2. Reform Judaism—
United States.   3. Jewish religious schools—United States.
I. Title.
BM103.H36   1997
296.6'8'0973—dc21   97–19889
                                                        CIP

Designed by Bill Frambes Typesetting
Typeset in Palatino by Bill Frambes Typesetting

The publication of this book was made possible
through generous grants from the

SAMUEL BRONFMAN FOUNDATION, INC.
and the

JEWISH EDUCATION SERVICE OF NORTH AMERICA.

Table of Contents

Acknowledgments

My journey toward this research began in a seminar on Jewish education offered by Professor Joseph Lukinsky at Brandeis University. It gained momentum at the Harvard Graduate School of Education where I studied with Professors Lawrence Kohlberg and Fred Erickson. My friend and colleague Ray McDermott has been a guide to my thinking about culture and ethnographies. Sam Heilman has been a model for combining ethnographic and Jewish interests.

Support for the first phase of this research was given by the Mandel Associated Foundations of Cleveland. I thank Mr. Mort Mandel and Professors Seymour Fox and Arthur Naparstak for that support.

Encouragement to write this book came at the right moment from my colleagues and friends Barry Holtz and Bernie Reisman. Barry helped me through the initial stages of conceptualization. Bernie kept me on track the whole way. My wonderful colleagues in the Hornstein Program and the Cohen Center have encouraged me from start to finish. Jonathan Sarna helped clarify some of the historical background for this research.

The Network for Research in Jewish Education has been a most supportive context in which to share my ideas as they have developed over the years. I thank my fellow researchers for their encouragement and feedback.

The time I spent at Stanford University with Professors Lee Shulman and Arnie Eisen and the doctoral students in Jewish Education, who provided me with a home away from home, proved invaluable for writing the second half of the book.

The rabbis and educators of Temple Akiba and Temple Hillel were far more than the subjects of this research. They were also collaborators in the research. They opened their doors to me and took me into their confidence. They shared their ideas and feelings and, in turn, helped me formulate my reactions to what I was observing. What I have written is my own and yet also the product of our joint venture. My debt to these Jewish educators is enormous.

My editor, Ellen Frankel, is another partner in this work. From the beginning Ellen believed in this project and over time has taught me to write a clearer and more focused prose. This book would never have seen the light of day without her editorial guidance. I also received much help with the manuscript from Jere Hinds and Naomi Bass of the Hornstein Program. They and Natalie Greene are the backup team on which I have relied.

Throughout this project I have been sustained by the rare and wondrous love of my wife, Gail, and daughters, Tamara and Ziva. They are the foundation for all I have achieved.

I dedicate this book to the memory of my father, Philip Reimer, and Gail's mother, Natalia Twersky. Their spirit lives with us as a blessing.

Foreword

by Jonathan Woocher

American Jews have a love-hate relationship with Jewish education.

Though precise figures are difficult to come by, the best estimates are that American Jews today spend more than $1.5 billion annually to maintain an educational system that includes nearly three thousand schools and thousands more educational programs held in a wide variety of institutional settings. This system involves close to fifty thousand teachers of all sorts and more than a million Jews who study regularly—almost half of them young people between the ages of three and eighteen. It is an impressive enterprise, especially when one considers that it is entirely voluntary. In particular, the commitment of American Jews to educate their children in the Jewish tradition appears to persist at a remarkable level: nearly three-quarters of all Jewish youth today will receive some Jewish education by the time they reach adulthood, a figure that has remained nearly constant for decades.

The recent wave of anxiety concerning the prospects of "Jewish continuity" in America has only heightened the hopes invested in Jewish education. For many active Jews, the proposition that Jewish education is the best, and perhaps the only, guarantor of Jewish survival in the face of assimilation has become axiomatic. The words of the blue-ribbon Commission on Jewish Education in North America in its 1991 report, *A Time to Act*, express a position heard today almost everywhere: "The responsibility for developing Jewish identity and instilling a commitment to Judaism . . . now rests primarily with education."

Happily, these are not idle hopes. Almost without exception, sociological studies of Jewish identity demonstrate that Jewish education does "work." Jews who have had more extensive and intensive Jewish educational experiences tend to have stronger Jewish identities than those who have had less or none at all. The logic of these findings has impressed funders as well: money is flowing into Jewish education, not least including from the growing number of private foundations that have become significant sources of "venture capital" for innovation and the development of whole new sub-fields, such as Jewish family education, during the past decade.

There is evidence, then, of a continuing, and perhaps even warming, romance between American Jews and Jewish education. But there is also evidence of an abiding dissatisfaction and discomfort with the Jewish education that many American Jews actually encounter. If Jewish education now benefits from the conviction that it is American Jewry's last, best bulwark against assimilation, it also suffers from a widespread perception of failure and mediocrity. There are those who ask sincerely whether pouring additional dollars into the very enterprise that has brought American Jewry to its current sorry condition is not a classic instance of Gresham's Law. Most unbiased observers would reject the contention that American Jewish education has been a "failure," but few would deny that it is beset with problems and is far less effective than it might, perhaps must, be.

Many would also doubt how committed to excellence in Jewish education American Jews really are. By and large, Jewish education in America is pediatric: the highest rates of participation are found among eleven and twelve year olds, just prior to the Bar or Bat Mitzvah ceremony that for many Jews marks the end of their formal Jewish education. For every Jewish adult who participates regularly in some form of Jewish study, nine do not. What is worse, many (if not most) American Jews do not even expect the experience of Jewish education to be a happy or rewarding one. Tales of long hours spent in painfully boring "Hebrew school" classes abound. "You'll go because I went" is the best reply many a resigned parent can muster when asked "Why do I have to go?" by a protesting child. Because the commitment of so many American Jews to Jewish education is less than wholehearted, there is a constant struggle to maintain standards of quality, to recruit and adequately remunerate educators, to fend off competitors (like Little League or ski vacations) for precious "leisure" time, and to convince anyone—students, parents, or teachers—that what goes on in Jewish classrooms genuinely matters.

In truth, American Jews have valued Jewish education as they value a vaccination. They have sent their children to Jewish schools in the hope that they would thereby be "inoculated" against the dread disease of "assimilationitis" later in life. And, like most vaccinations, they have expected the experience to be relatively brief, largely passive, somewhat painful, and administered by experts who possess arcane knowledge that the average patient does not need to possess. This level of Jewish "health-mindedness" is not to be scorned. The mass participation in Jewish schooling that it has nurtured and sustained is a notable achievement. (And today, a significant minority of Jewish families does choose to administer a somewhat more substantial dose of Jewish study to their children in day schools.) But the paradigm is outmoded and, increasingly, it just doesn't work. Inoculatory Jewish education may have been "good enough" when social boundaries and ethnic memories kept Jews "in the fold" as a natural consequence of their birth. But clearly, the prophylactic effects of a minimalist education have been wearing off. The vaccine, at least in the dosage that many American Jews receive, has lost its potency.

Confronted by this reality, Jewish educational leadership in America—and a significant number of rank and file American Jews—have made a decisive choice. They have rejected the old paradigm of Jewish education as a vaccination and have begun to create a new one. In a myriad of ways, Jewish institutions and educators are struggling to redesign, reposition, and revitalize Jewish education. They are striving to justify American Jewry's abiding, though often disappointed, faith in its importance by making

Jewish education more compelling, inspiring, and satisfying, at once more relevant and more significant for contemporary American Jews. The new paradigm—one of Jewish education as lifelong "wellness"—is not yet fully enshrined. But its outlines are visible, and the struggle to enact it in a variety of modes and settings for a diverse population is the most exciting and important one taking place in the world of Jewish education today.

Joseph Reimer's *Succeeding at Jewish Education: How One Synagogue Made It Work* is an account of how one synagogue is in fact putting this new paradigm into place. It is, as Professor Reimer vividly demonstrates, a dramatic story, with bold characters, a tension-ridden plot, themes that resonate well beyond the immediate stage on which it is set, and important lessons for all who are interested in the future of Jewish education. It is an inspiring story, not because it is unique or depicts unalloyed triumph, but precisely because what happened at Temple Akiba *could* happen elsewhere. Like so many Jewish institutions today, Temple Akiba finds itself traversing a narrow ridge, seeking to move toward the twenty-first century while upholding a commitment to openness and diversity on the one hand and to an intensifying relationship with Jewish tradition on the other. And, despite (or perhaps because of) occasional sidesteps and even stumbles, it is walking along that ridge successfully; it is educating Jews and it is creating a Jewish community.

For those who believe in Jewish education's vital significance but fear for its ability to be effective in today's American environment, this is important news indeed. It is doubly important because Reimer chose to explore the possibilities and problems of Jewish education in the institution where these are most urgently on display: the synagogue. There can be little doubt that for American Jews, the synagogue is *the* preeminent "educating institution." As it has developed over the past half-century, most aspects of American Jewish education, including supplementary schooling (still the predominant form of Jewish education for children, despite the recent growth of all-day schools) and the education of Jewish youth and adults have become synagogue-centered.

This marriage has not been without its critics. The all-too-evident weaknesses of the Jewish education that many synagogues provide for both children and adults have led to repeated calls over the decades for radical structural reforms that would challenge the preeminence of the synagogue in Jewish education. By and large, however, these calls have fallen on deaf ears, for which, in retrospect, we should be grateful. For while no institution can or should enjoy a monopoly over any form of Jewish education, the centrality of the synagogue in the education system is a potential boon of enormous importance. At its best, the synagogue, more than any other Jewish institution, can be a true "educating community," where the Judaism that is taught is at the same time practiced, where Jewish children and especially Jewish adults, can not only study Torah together, but pray and perform *mitzvot* together. No factor is more critical for the ultimate success of Jewish education than that it be anchored in the life of a real community of Jews, and there is no institution better suited to creating such a community than the synagogue. Indeed, perhaps the greatest challenge in liberating Jewish education from the "old" vaccination paradigm is to sunder the instrumental connection between education and identity (i.e., Jewish study is good because it leads to Jewish identity) in order to restore a more authentic relationship in which Jewish study is an intrinsic expression and constitutive component of both Jewish identity and community—it is what Jews do to *be*, not just to *become*, Jewish.

How difficult this challenge is, and yet that it is possible to make headway despite the difficulties, is the chastening but hopeful lesson that emerges from Reimer's artful and insightful ethnography of Temple Akiba. The key, he shows us, lies in the "distinctive Torah"—the special style or approach to the study and celebration of Judaism—that is taught and enacted in this community. What makes this Torah effective for Temple Akiba's congregants and their children is its ability to build a bridge for them between the truths of their lives and those of the Jewish tradition as it has been taught in the past. The bridge is at times shaky. Indeed, at some points, it fails to materialize at all. But the work goes on, led by the rabbinic-educational team that has taken up the challenge, and the connection is made again and again.

Temple Akiba is a "liberal" religious institution. Its "Torah" goes farther than would that of many more "conservative" synagogues in accommodating diverse family structures and lifestyles, contemporary aesthetics, moral and intellectual freedom, and selectivity vis-à-vis the received body of traditional Jewish values and practices. Yet, though Temple Akiba's place along the spectrum of traditionalism may be fairly far to the left, it is difficult to imagine that any but the most Orthodox synagogues could "do" Jewish education effectively today in a fundamentally different way. Temple Akiba's rabbis have succeeded in introducing an approach to Jewish learning that strives to be genuinely dialogic. The learner is never asked to give up the standpoint of her/his own experience and thoughtful reflection as the ultimate criterion for making truth claims. But she/he is encouraged to look into the texts of the tradition for the experiences and reflections contained therein as well, and to accord these the same respect as potentially truth-bearing as one accords one's own. This is a prescription for Jewish education that is serious, that requires hard work from both teacher and student and that will occasionally provoke disagreement and discontent. But, as Reimer illustrates, it is also a Jewish education that can actually reach Jews and help them see Torah as relevant and contemporary, without being trite and faddish.

Reimer tells us that he set out to write one kind of book, but ended up writing something rather different. His original goal was to understand why some Hebrew schools (i.e., supplementary educational programs sponsored by synagogues) "work," when so many others (as noted above) are perceived as ineffective and even counterproductive. His initial research confirmed that a key variable was the extent to which the congregation provided a supportive and nurturing environment for its school. This finding alone provides a powerful lens through which to re-view the question of how to help Jewish education live up to its promise.

But the implications of Reimer's narrative and analysis in this book extend well beyond the issue of effective Jewish schooling. At Temple Akiba, we see that it is not the school that shapes the "distinctive Torah" that it teaches; it is the community as a whole. (The school, in fact, turns out to be a somewhat problematic arena in which to transmit this Torah, both because some of the students resist, shy away from, or are simply incapable of taking the risks of "bridge-building," and because more of the "old" paradigm of Jewish education as involuntary vaccination survives in this setting.) However, even this formulation does not go far enough. By introducing "dramatic performance" as a way of understanding what is happening in the life of Temple Akiba, Reimer recasts the role of educational activity and decisions in a striking—and Jewishly significant—way. The challenge that Temple Akiba's leaders and members face is whether the "distinctive Torah" they teach *will*, in fact, be the Torah they live by. This question reappears in a variety of contexts and settings, from a family education session to a dispute over instituting mandatory Hebrew studies in the school. It is a challenge because the core values of Temple Akiba's "distinctive Torah" are not in seamless harmony with one another. This synagogue wishes to be profoundly respectful of the individual and of Jewish tradition; it seeks to be maximally open and to uphold standards of Jewish knowledge and competency. As we see in this book, this is easier said than done.

What we also see, though, is that in striving to meet this challenge, Temple Akiba becomes a Torah-affirming community. Only because it does take its teaching seriously can the values it articulates really merit being called *Torah*. The very act of trying to be faithful to these values, even when they are in tension with one another, is the signal that this is an institution where Jewish education truly matters. The playing out of the conflicts, whether in a class section or a committee meeting, is a ritual performance in the best sense: it enables Temple Akiba to reaffirm its identity and its distinctive Torah as something deep and fundamental to the life of the institution, something that provides meaning and purpose, something that defines the community.

What we encounter in *Succeeding at Jewish Education: How One Synagogue Makes It Work* is, therefore, an "educating congregation" in two senses: it is a congregation that places the Jewish educational mission at the heart of its self-definition, and it is also a congregation that allows the education that takes place within it to shape its evolving culture, contents, and identity. There is no perfection here, neither in the synagogue community nor in its leaders nor in the teaching and learning going on. But there is Torah, and there is the struggle to create a community that both generates and is transformed by its relationship to Jewish teaching and tradition.

Reimer readily acknowledges the limits of ethnography as a window through which to view a broad landscape. Temple Akiba is probably typical of nothing, but it is indicative of a great deal, thanks primarily to the discerning eye that Reimer casts upon it. This is the battlefield where the future of American Judaism will be played out. If synagogues like Temple Akiba can forge, teach, and enact a distinctive Torah that makes Judaism a force, or at least a factor, in shaping the answers individuals give to the central questions in their lives, then Judaism will do well. If its bridge-building endeavors ultimately fail, or if the tensions among its values and members prove more acute than a community can sustain, then the future of American Jewry is surely cloudy at best.

It is time for American Jews to put their love-hate relationship with Jewish education and the old paradigm that sustained it into the past. Beyond romanticization, beyond recrimination, lies the challenging but rewarding work of studying Torah and living Torah. At Temple Akiba, this is happening, sometimes in traditional, sometimes in quite modern ways. And, if it can happen there, it can happen elsewhere. Thanks to Joseph Reimer we can now understand far better not only what can happen, but how and why, in the drama of contemporary Jewish education. This is a considerable gift, for which we should be deeply grateful.

Jonathan Woocher

Succeeding at Jewish Education

Chapter 1
The Educating Synagogue

Jewish learning and living in our open society require a bounded space to enclose and protect the germ of Jewish activity. The communal response has been to build "Jewish spaces" in the midst of the most open and secular society in which Jews have ever lived.

This book is an exploration of one such space, the synagogue. American Jews have asked their synagogues to fulfill more vital functions than any other communal agency. In comparison to the Israeli synagogue, which is heavily government-funded and serves primarily the ritual needs of the Orthodox community, the American synagogue is a privately funded, volunteer organization that serves the ritual, social, and educational needs of a broad spectrum of American Jewry. Mordecai Kaplan correctly understood, as early as the 1930s, that the American synagogue would be developing into a community center rather than remaining predominantly a house of worship.[1]

Of all the functions of the synagogue, none is as demanding as that of providing Jewish education to the community. There is a long record of synagogues functioning as houses of study, but the American synagogue has taken this tradition to new lengths. In no other Jewish community around the world does the local synagogue provide the primary Jewish education to everyone from tots in the nursery school to the elderly in adult education. Nowhere else does the synagogue provide the classrooms, teachers, and curriculum for the majority of school-age children who come to learn Hebrew and Judaica in the years before, and sometimes after, their Bar or Bat Mitzvah.[2]

There is a common perception, backed by an array of statistics, that many synagogues do not do well in fulfilling their educational function. The "Hebrew school" or "supplementary school" run by the synagogue has not fared well in either popular or scholarly depictions.[3] Yet, generations of American Jewish parents have turned to the local synagogue to provide their school-age children with a basic Jewish education. They do so for a period of four to ten years per child at considerable cost to the family.

A paradox is embedded in this relationship between Jewish parents and their local synagogues. Compared to their Christian neighbors, American Jews are far less involved in religious practice. Also, fewer Jews profess belief in the supernatural or the afterlife, and fewer belong to or attend houses of worship. Yet, when it comes to the religious education of their children, Jews in surprising numbers line up to register their children at the synagogue school.[4] How is this possible?

Some have suggested that many Jews practice a life-cycle-based religion: during certain stretches of the life cycle, they are mostly indifferent to religion. But when beginning a family, many feel mysteriously drawn back to the religion of their ancestors. They feel less drawn to change their private beliefs or personal practices than to transmit their heritage to the next generation. Often, even nonpracticing Jews feel intensely guilty at the thought of their children not being raised as Jews. Since they lack the personal resources to transmit Jewishness on their own, they turn to the synagogue for help in educating their children.[5]

Undoubtedly, American synagogues benefit from this arrangement. Parents of children are far more likely to join synagogues than are adults without children.[6] But this pattern does set up a potentially odd relationship between the synagogue and these members. How do the two sides find a common language? What do essentially secular Jews have to say to rabbis and Jewish educators? What do the synagogue professionals have to say to either parents or children whose home lives in most ways do not reflect traditional Jewish practice?

These are questions that have intrigued and impelled

me to undertake the study reported in this book. Much has been written about the formal education of children in synagogue schools. Less has been written about the synagogue as a religious and social institution. But almost nothing has been written about the educating synagogue: the ways that the American synagogue presents its Judaic mission to its constituency. Few scholars have thought systematically about this relationship—of how the religiously committed synagogue leadership and the majority of members who do not share those commitments are actively engaged in trying to communicate with and understand one another.

I bring to this study a slightly different understanding of Jewish education than is found elsewhere in the literature. Most who have written about Jewish education in the synagogue have focused on the instruction of children, adults, and families in Jewish knowledge, skills, and values. They have focused on the formal and informal educational programs used to convey these subjects to the students.[7]

I affirm the importance of this approach, but take another tack. I begin with Schoem's observation that in entering a synagogue, most American Jews are "stepping out" of the normal routines of their lives.[8] I then imagine what it might be like for someone who considers himself or herself a Jew to walk into this Jewish space and discover that it requires participation in a set of ritual and educational activities that feel foreign. Such a person might wonder: "If I feel Jewish, why does being in a synagogue feel so distant from who I am?"

In our culture there are two quite distinct ways of defining oneself as a Jew. One way is primarily ethnic and secular and arises from the experience of being "other," of not being Christian in Christian America. This is the Jewishness so powerfully portrayed in Woody Allen's films and Philip Roth's fiction. But the second sense of Jewishness arises from an attachment to Jewish religious traditions, including lighting the Sabbath candles, celebrating the Passover seder, and singing Hebrew songs.

For many Jews these two ways of defining oneself as a Jew overlap and intermix. Study after empirical study indicate, however, that while the ethnic sense of being Jewish continues to survive among many American Jews, the number of Jews who are regularly involved in the religious practices of Judaism continues to slip. Not only does the number who are at all religiously involved decline, but of those involved, the number who participate in regular, weekly religious practices also continues to decline.[9]

Synagogues, of course, are in the business of promoting regular religious practice; yet such practice is the very way of defining oneself as a Jew that is losing most ground. One would therefore expect to see business dropping off for many synagogues—and this is generally the case, with one important exception: among families with school-age children who continue to join in higher numbers.[10]

Of the parents who join synagogues, there must be many who think of themselves primarily as ethnic Jews and who wish to pass that identity on to their children. In sending their children to the synagogue, however, they enter into contact with the religious definition of Jewishness. At that moment a dialogue may develop between these parents and the rabbi and educator over what is involved in being Jewish today in America.

My hope in undertaking this study was to eavesdrop on that conversation to better understand the dialogue that surrounds the Jewish education of children in synagogues. For I am in basic agreement with Isa Aron who, in a seminal paper, called into question the identification of *Jewish education* with *instruction in Judaism*. Recognizing that the teaching that goes on in classrooms is only a small part of the whole Jewish educational program, Aron suggests expanding our vision of synagogue education to include the "enculturation" of Jews to the basic experiences of Jewish living. If in coming to the synagogue both children and parents are stepping out of the normal routines of their lives, the education that they receive needs to walk them through some of the basic Jewish experiences that define a person as a religious Jew.[11]

But I wish to go a step beyond Aron's argument. In her view it is the synagogue, through its professional leadership, that enculturates the family into Jewish living by involving them in Jewish learning and experience. That view, in which the synagogue acts upon the family members to change some aspects of their lives, assumes a one-way direction of influence. I would suggest the influence is actually two-way. By becoming involved, the families bring to the synagogue their own set of issues and understandings of what it means to be Jewish in our times. They are not a blank slate upon which the synagogue inscribes its brand of Judaism. Rather, they are active partners in a dialogue who feel entitled to influence as well as to be influenced.[12]

Jewish education is a two-way or, actually, a multidirectional process in which teachers and learners are engaged in influencing one another. While teachers and learners do not bring equal knowledge or experience to this process, and while the official responsibility of providing the Jewish education lies with the synagogue, the power equation between teachers and students in this voluntary context can shift very quickly. This shift can occur because the paradigms of knowledge that the synagogue offers are not dominant in American culture, and Jewish educators are often teaching against the grain of the culture. To capture student interest—to be credible in their students' eyes—Jewish educators often have to concede some of their power to the dominant issues of the day. Whether it is discussing sports or sex, Vietnam, or Bosnia, Jewish educators are always mixing metaphors to stay current with their students' lives.

The synagogue is always vying for influence. Having no governmental mandate, no deep pockets of financial support, and not even a majority of Jews as members, the synagogue scrambles for its position within American society. Jewish education, more than religious services or any other social activity, is the synagogue's main drawing card. It affords the synagogue its primary opportunity to develop a lasting relationship with much of its constituency. How the synagogue handles that relationship may be a key to its prospects for survival and, certainly, for its flourishing.

The Travails of Hebrew School

It is no secret that all has not gone well in the synagogue's relationship with the children who attend the school and the parents who send them. There is perhaps no better known depiction of this failure than in Philip Roth's early short story, "The Conversion of the Jews."[13]

Set in a synagogue basement classroom in the 1940s, the story introduces the thirteen-year-old Ozzie Freedman, his friend Itzie, and their teacher, Rabbi Binder. A serious but challenging student, Ozzie raises the kind of questions that Rabbi Binder does not always appreciate. Among those is the one about the birth of Jesus.

> "He was a real person, Jesus, but he wasn't like God, and we don't believe he is God." Slowly, Ozzie was explaining Rabbi Binder's position to Itzie, who had been absent from Hebrew school the previous afternoon.
> "The Catholics," Itzie said helpfully, "they believe in Jesus Christ, that he's God. . . ."
> "His mother was Mary, and his father probably was Joseph," Ozzie said. "But the New Testament says his real father was God."
> "His *real* father?"
> "Yeah," Ozzie said, "that's the big thing, his father's supposed to be God."
> "Bull."

Roth wonderfully captures the rough appreciation these Jewish boys might have had of the Christian world and, especially, of the Virgin Birth. But to ask about these matters could lead only to trouble, as Ozzie reports to Itzie.

> "I asked the question about God, how if He could create the heaven and earth in six days, and make . . . the light in six days . . . why couldn't He let a woman have a baby without having intercourse."

Ozzie may have thought he was asking about God,

but, he adds, Rabbi Binder "starts screaming that I was deliberately simple-minded and a wise guy and that my mother had to come, and this was the last time."

Matters grow only worse the following Wednesday afternoon when Rabbi Binder, during the free discussion hour, insists that a reluctant Ozzie "rise to his feet and give the class the advantage of his thoughts." Ozzie hesitantly repeats his question. A commotion arises in response, and as the teacher turns to see what happened,

> Ozzie shouted into the rabbi's back what he couldn't have shouted to his face . . .
> "You don't know! You don't know anything about God!"
> The rabbi spun back towards Ozzie. "What?"
> "You don't know—you don't—"
> "Apologize, Oscar, apologize!" It was a threat.
> "You don't—"
> Rabbi Binder's hand flicked out at Ozzie's cheek. Perhaps it had only been meant to clamp the boy's mouth shut, but Ozzie ducked and the palm caught him squarely on the nose.
> The blood came in a short, red spurt on to Ozzie's shirt front.

All hell breaks loose. Ozzie runs from the classroom with Rabbi Binder and the class in hot pursuit and races to the synagogue roof, where he locks the door. The scene on the roof is a drama of boy against teacher wherein Rabbi Binder's assumption that Ozzie might jump to his death reverses the power equation. Now the rabbi has transgressed and must make confession. Ozzie has the rabbi, his mother, and classmates down on their knees confessing, "God can make a child without intercourse."

A fictional Roth story is clearly not a mirror to social reality and certainly not a sociology of classroom life. Only Roth could imagine a confessional scene of these proportions. Yet the drama that this story portrays and the themes that it captures in comical form ring true to the concerns of scholars who have studied the realities of synagogue education.[14] More broadly, they ring true to a reading audience familiar with the travails of a Hebrew school education. For Roth's story reflects a commonly held perception that this education is not serious, the teachers are often ill-prepared, and the students all too often are passing time rather than learning matters of consequence.

Nonetheless, I cannot read this story without wincing. While enjoying Roth's comedy, I also hear the serious side to Ozzie's unanswered question. He wants to know about God, about why a Jew would consider the Virgin Birth to be more beyond God's capacity than creating heaven and earth. Each time I read Binder's response I wonder: Is there no alternative to this pedagogic defensiveness? Is there no room in synagogues for questions like these? Is this what Hebrew school was created to be?

Most of us who went to Hebrew school have little idea of why or how it was created. We know it is tied up with becoming a Bar or Bat Mitzvah, but the rest is vague. Mostly, we are glad not to think about it until we too have children and the prospect of their education raises the question anew.

I differ from most of my peers in not having let go of these experiences even after growing up. I attended Hebrew school for only two years before my parents transferred me to a Jewish day school. There I encountered teachers not unlike Roth's fictional Rabbi Binder. I, too, had my face slapped for the questions I asked and felt at times like jumping from the school's roof. Yet I also came away with a love for the Judaica I was taught—a love I feel each time I open a Hebrew text. Still, I wonder to this day how I can love that which I once dreaded. How can an Ozzie Freedman grow to be an adult who still cares to ask about God?

This very personal question has led to this study of synagogue education. As a developmental psychologist with an interest in education and a training in ethnographic methodology, I had completed studies of kibbutz education in Israel and alternative high schools in Massachusetts.[15] I wanted to return to my native experience, to my own Jewish education, yet I wanted to do so in a way that would be consistent with my professional training as a social scientist and informative for my peers—Jews and Christians—who, like myself, may be wondering: Can it be different? Can religious education be truly educational—substantive and enabling—rather than vapid and repressive?

My challenge was to find a synagogue setting that I could study with the systematic attentiveness of a social scientist but also the hopefulness of one seeking an alternative to Rabbi Binder and all that he imaginatively represents.

Entering the Field

Having posed a broad research question, I had to develop a research plan to gather data on a Jewish educational setting. I was looking for a synagogue rather than a Jewish day school and planned to do an ethnographic study based on participatory observation rather than on surveys and questionnaires.

I knew I was hardly a disinterested observer. Having grown up in an Orthodox Jewish home in Queens, New York, and attended both a synagogue and day school, I had strong feelings on the subject. In choosing to write an ethnography, rather than an autobiography, I would have to exercise particular discipline in observing and analyzing events. I would have to be attentive to my personal reactions—and share them when relevant—but also capable of separating those reactions from the events being reported. I would be walking a fine line between subjective reaction and disciplined observation—a line every ethnographer has to walk.[16]

How was I to find the synagogue or synagogues to study? I began by selecting a single metropolitan Jewish community in which I already had connections. To learn more about Jewish education in that metropolitan area, I interviewed ten communal leaders and asked them to share their perceptions of synagogues and synagogue education.[17] From those interviews I learned much about this Jewish community, but four main points stand out:

1. From the leaders' perspectives this is a community in which Jewish education has enjoyed wide communal support. The education is varied and includes not only schools for children but also summer camps, youth programs, adult and family education, and Jewish services for college students and young adults.

2. Jewish day school education has been growing more rapidly than synagogue education and enjoying much communal support. At the same time, synagogues have been gaining new communal support for Jewish family education through programs for the parents and families of children attending the synagogue school.

3. There is a wide range of quality among synagogue educational programs. Some synagogues have reputations for supporting high-quality educational programs, while others place much less importance on educational programming. In the extreme, some synagogue boards treat their school as a drain on the synagogue's financial resources.

4. Synagogue education is not all of one piece. A given synagogue may have a strong religious school but a weak youth program. Another may place special emphasis on education for adults. Just a few synagogues enjoy the reputation for having excellent educational programs across the board.

Of all these points, my attention was drawn to the last one: If there were a few synagogues with the reputation for maintaining broad educational excellence, what distinguished them from the rest? What allowed them this distinction? From these initial interviews I gleaned a few hints. Above all, I became curious to learn more about these reputedly distinctive synagogues.

To identify these distinctive synagogues, I approached eight professionals with expertise in the area of Jewish education.[18] I asked each in a telephone interview if there were any synagogues with "especially good educational programs," and if so, could he or she identify them.

All eight believed there were such synagogues, and in total they identified ten. Of the ten, one was selected by every respondent; another by all but one. The other eight were nominated fewer times.

Given this degree of consensus, I thought I had the synagogue sites I sought. But there was a problem: both the synagogues named were from the Reform movement. If I were to choose to study two synagogues, I would have preferred that one be Conservative and the other Reform to reflect the diversity of synagogues within the Jewish community.[19] On further reflection, though, I decided that if these experts—who came from diverse Jewish backgrounds—selected these two as having "especially good educational programs," I would stick with their recommendations. They did not introduce denominational status as a determining factor and neither would I.[20]

I had another reason for preferring to study a Reform synagogue. Since my college years I had considerable involvement with institutions in the Conservative movement. I thought I knew this movement fairly well, but I was almost totally new to the Reform movement. That felt like an advantage. In working as an ethnographer I was committed to seeing the familiar through new eyes—that is, I was committed to looking for underlying cultural and social patterns not obvious to the casual observer. Perhaps in a Reform context, in which these patterns would be less familiar, I would be less likely to take things for granted and feel freer to look beyond the given social order to inquire how it came to be as it now appears.

These were all theoretical considerations until I met the educators at these synagogues. It was they who would finally convince me to study these sites.

The Educators, My Informants

After the High Holidays, I made my first appointments to meet with Rabbi Don Marcus of Temple Akiba and Ms. Sally Tessler of Temple Hillel.[21] I had met each of them previously but knew them only casually. Now I would be asking for a major commitment.

It is hard to describe what an ethnographer is really asking when first contacting educators like these. On the surface the ethnographer is asking to conduct research in their domain. But, in contrast to a researcher who interviews or surveys people and then leaves the scene, an ethnographer sticks around. He or she is asking the educator: Would you mind if I spent considerable time hanging around your space, observing, taking notes, asking questions, blending into the background? Would you be willing to become my informant: letting me into your work, your life, and your way of thinking and feeling about who you are and what you do?[22] Clearly this is a major request. In truth, I could not have asked all that of Rabbi Marcus and Ms. Tessler during those first interviews; instead I asked for much less.

I had planned this study in two phases. The first would be more exploratory than the second. I would be preparing the ground during the first year, 1989–1990, by simply getting to know these synagogues and their schools through observations and interviews. By the end of the spring of 1990, I would write a portrait of the two synagogue schools that would attempt to answer the question: Are these schools alternatives to the usual negative portrait of Hebrew schools? Once that sketch was completed,[23] the educators and I could decide whether to proceed to a second phase of a more complete ethnographic study.

Yet, it did not take me long to develop a special sense about these two people. Here were two professionally and personally secure educators who could tolerate the company and scrutiny of an outside observer. Here were two people who would allow me entry into their schools and welcome me into their confidence. In my search for informants—culturally aware insiders who would reflectively guide me through their worlds—I found what I wanted in Don Marcus and Sally Tessler. Once we began working together and trusting each other, these two parallel relationships developed and grew in a way that nourished the work of this ethnography.

The Two Synagogue Sites

Temple Akiba and Temple Hillel are both similar and dissimilar to one another. They are modern Reform congregations, liberal in orientation, and quite seriously engaged in reincorporating traditional Jewish practices into their worship and study. Both are located in the same metropolitan area and draw primarily upper-middle-class professional families for their membership.

But they differ in terms of location, size, and history. Temple Akiba is a large urban congregation, while Temple Hillel is a medium-size suburban congregation. Dating back to the nineteenth century, Temple Akiba has played a historic role in the development of the local Jewish community and the national Reform movement. It wears its history proudly, if problematically. Temple Hillel was founded only in the late 1950s, when Jews were moving rapidly into the suburbs, and it still counts many of its founders as current members. Temple Hillel is less self-consciously denominational than is Temple Akiba. It also has far fewer elderly members.

With over 1,700 members, Temple Akiba has a large, full-time staff of three rabbis, a cantor, and an executive director.[24] One of the rabbis, Don Marcus, serves as the temple educator. As temple educator, he is responsible for administering the school, with 450 students in kindergarten through twelfth grade, a 30-person staff, and the informal youth programs. With approximately 660 members, Temple Hillel employs a smaller full-time staff of two rabbis, one temple educator, and an administrator. Sally Tessler, the temple educator, administers the K–12 school of 300 students and 15 faculty members. The younger rabbi oversees the informal youth program and serves as youth director to members in high school. In both congregations the clergy teach in the school and are involved with the youth program. Both have very active programs of adult and family education as well as outreach programs to interfaith couples and non-Jews who are considering conversion.

I chose to study two synagogues to establish some

basis of comparison. These two temples have enough in common that when differences emerge, they stand out. I would learn how differences in history, location, and style have shaped the different congregational cultures, and how these congregational differences translate into varying emphases in the educational programs. I was interested in viewing each congregation as a whole and in seeing how education at all levels permeated the culture of each.

With that interest in mind, I spent November to May making my initial acquaintance with the two synagogues. I did a series of observations in the two schools, read all the documents available on the synagogues and schools, and spent a lot of my time talking with the two educators and the two senior rabbis. By May I had written my preliminary portrait based on what I had heard, read, and seen. The portrait was positive in tone and, based on the limited evidence I had, concluded that in these two synagogues one could find examples of "good synagogue schools."[25]

When I had completed phase one, I was convinced this portrait covered only the surface of the story. I had looked at how these synagogues generously support their religious schools, but I had not considered the broader question of how the synagogues themselves function as educational institutions: how they are constantly presenting themselves and the Judaism they represent to adults as well as to children. To gain a deeper understanding of how education at all levels fits into the cultures of these congregations, I would have to undertake a fuller ethnographic study of these synagogues the following year.

From Portrait to Ethnography

I would hardly be the first to write an ethnography of American synagogue life,[26] but my study would differ by looking at how contemporary synagogues educated their members. I would need to examine the religious school within the context of the synagogue's educational work with youth, adults, and families. I would examine how the school was run by the educator, as well as how the rabbis, cantor, and lay leaders were involved in educational policy-setting and practice throughout the synagogue.

I was well aware that I had chosen to study not the "average" synagogue but two that were singled out as exceptional. This choice might limit the generalizability of my findings. I was less concerned with identifying the factors that would account globally for success in synagogue education, however, than with telling the story of how a synagogue operates as an educational institution—for I had not seen that story told in any convincing detail.

The closest model was David Schoem's ethnography of a synagogue school. The great strength of his ethnography was to clarify the connection between what happens in the synagogue school and how Jews generally function in the context of American Jewish life. Schoem claims that by examining the myths that animate the life of the school and the parental expectations for the school, it becomes clear that the synagogue school *cannot* accomplish its educational goals. In his observation, many parents send their children to the synagogue school with conflicting wishes. They hope that the school will convey some sense of Jewish life to their children—but without threatening the secular rhythms of their suburban life. They want their children to meet and befriend other Jewish children, but not to the exclusion of developing many other social contacts. They want their children to learn enough Hebrew and Jewish content to be eligible for Bar and Bat Mitzvah, but the parents are not actually concerned with the quality of instruction and learning in the school.

One of the most powerful of Schoem's quotes comes from a parent who is explaining why he is not concerned about the quality of Jewish education his son Eddie is receiving.

> On occasion Eddie has told me he hates Hebrew school, and I say, "Edward, that's wonderful. You're carrying on a Jewish tradition. Because when I went to Hebrew school, I hated it, too. Because all good Jews hate Hebrew school."(p. 54)

If all good Jews hate Hebrew schools, one can appreciate the thin ice on which these schools skate. In Schoem's view, this parental attitude prevents the possibility of this school's making Judaism meaningful to children. Indeed, the classroom observations reported in his ethnography confirm his negative prognosis.

Schoem's study set the challenge for mine. Having found his ethnography convincing, how could I say that no one had adequately described the synagogue as an educational institution? Is that not what Schoem had done in his sobering portrait of the Shalom Synagogue and school?

I think not. Schoem accurately subtitled his book *An Ethnography of a Jewish Afternoon School.* Of course Schoem was aware that this Jewish afternoon school was sponsored by the Shalom Synagogue. In his description Schoem indicates the role that the rabbi and board play in setting policy for the school. But none of that holds his attention. His lens resembles Roth's; both richly capture the absurdity of the educational moment without attending to the organizational context in which the class or school is located.

I begin my work with the bold premise that the synagogue as context can make a difference. While there is no disproving Schoem's work, I hope to show not all synagogues are alike. I will explore the proposition that if the lay leadership of a synagogue is committed to making Jewish education a high priority, they—together with the educator and clergy—can create an educational environment in which "all good Jews" do *not* "hate Hebrew school."

In a meeting of the Shalom Synagogue's board of directors that Schoem attended, the members expressed deep uncertainty about the role of Jewish education in their congregation. When a debate arose over educational funding—as happens in most American synagogues—Schoem found that board members questioned whether quality education was a goal for their synagogue. One board member put the matter rather bluntly: "Does the congregation really want quality education? Maybe we just want kids to make it through their Bar Mitzvah?" (p. 72).

My preliminary research had convinced me that that

question had long ago been settled for the boards of the two synagogues I was studying. They were clear that the future of their synagogue will depend on the quality of the educational programs. While they continually debate the specifics of financing, they would no sooner cut the basic support for the school than they would deny their own children the money needed to attend a first-rate college or university.

But my interest went beyond financing the school. I thought I had found in Temple Akiba and Temple Hillel congregations that also take Jewish education seriously as an activity for adults and families. For these two synagogues the term *Jewish education* is not synonymous with *Hebrew school;* it encompasses the larger congregation. One could observe in these synagogues that children are not the only ones with books in hand and lessons to complete. The educators and rabbis work with both children and adults and express the view that if Jewish learning is to be taken seriously, it must be engaged in by members of all ages.

None of those aspects of synagogue education appears in Schoem's work. Whether they exist at the Shalom Synagogue is hard to tell. But they did seem to exist in Temple Akiba and Temple Hillel, which is why I chose them as sites. Then, having chosen these sites for closer study, I had to go beyond surface comparisons to ask: Do differences of expressed educational policy actually show up in observations of daily practice? I now had to inquire whether—or to what extent—the differences I *sensed* between these two temples and Schoem's Shalom Synagogue were actually observable in the daily operations of the educators, the attitudes of the parents, and the behavior of the children. I had to entertain the null hypothesis that beneath the rhetorical surface of interviews I had conducted and the policy statements I had read, there was a daily reality that did not differ much from the sad state of affairs that Schoem describes in his ethnography.

With these questions in mind, I took the first steps of consulting with the educators and senior rabbis of Temple Akiba and Temple Hillel. My request to return for another year of intensive field study was approved by all these individuals. None felt this research would need the approval of their boards of directors, and I did not seek it.

I began this second, more intensive phase of research in August and continued with it through the following June. Employing a fuller ethnographic methodology than time allowed in phase one, I spent many hours observing school classes from kindergarten through high school and talking to the teaching staff of each school. I also attended worship services, adult education classes, and outreach sessions in both congregations. At Temple Akiba I was invited to attend a meeting of the board of the congregation and to observe the monthly meetings of the religious school committee on a regular basis. At Temple Hillel I was invited to attend the semimonthly family education sessions conducted by the assistant rabbi. In both congregations I conducted several hour-long interviews with each of the four rabbis and the two presidents of the synagogues. I conducted formal interviews with each of the synagogue educators on several occasions and spoke with them on an informal basis almost every week. The educators were my primary informants throughout the research.

Although I had considerable informal contact with both children and parents, I decided not to interview or survey these two groups of participants formally. In budgeting my time, I decided to learn what I could from observing children and parents in the school and synagogue but to tell this story primarily from the perspective of the rabbis, educators, and teachers. I set out to learn as much as I could about how the professionals perceived the mission of the synagogue and its school and then balance those perceptions against what I observed in the classrooms of the school and the sanctuaries of the synagogue. The one important exception to this focus came in observing the meetings of the religious school committee of Temple Akiba, where I had considerable opportunity to hear how ten exceptionally committed parents viewed both their congregation and the school.

During my observations, I tried to listen as unobtrusively as I could in order to minimize my interference with the process under way. My note-taking could not have gone unnoticed, however. The feedback I received on my presence was positive but telling. I always felt welcome and included, but at times teachers or laypeople would politely but firmly ask that I not enter their space. At other times the educators or teachers would comment on how strange it was that I observed and listened to them, while they never knew what I was thinking or how I was evaluating what I saw. The lack of immediate feedback was somewhat unnerving to them.

After a time I felt I blended into the environment. In many ways I am not unlike the parents and professionals who populate these synagogues, so my presence was not unusual. Because of my own Jewish background, however, being in Reform congregations was for me like entering a new culture. Not that the people were unfamiliar, but the assumptions governing the religious behavior of the synagogues were. I devoted much time and effort to trying to understand the Judaism practiced in these congregations. Undoubtedly that effort will convince some and disturb others. But it was an important part of my learning, particularly when I had to wrestle to balance my subjective reactions with my professional perspective as a researcher.

As the study progressed, I moved back and forth between the two synagogues. This was made easier by their maintaining somewhat different educational schedules. However, as ethnographer, my attention was not evenly divided. I was being emotionally drawn more deeply into the life of Temple Akiba than Temple Hillel. There is no simple way to explain why this occurred. But once I realized it, I made a fateful decision to make my work in Temple Akiba the foreground of this ethnography and use my work at Temple Hillel as background. That decision is reflected in the writing of this book. Readers will be introduced more fully to the life of Temple Akiba and references to Temple Hillel will be sparse.

A Dramatic Perspective on Synagogue Life

After completing the year of intensive fieldwork and reading through the volumes of notes I had taken, I was struck by an emerging theme. While neither synagogue had experienced a major crisis, both experienced one or more "mini-crises" that were directly related to the educational mission of the synagogue. By *mini-crisis* I mean a series of events in which a public clash of opinion develops among parties in the synagogue over an emotionally charged issue. These clashes did not result in anyone's losing a job or in numbers of congregants leaving the congregation. Yet, these mini-crises illustrated how intensely emotions surrounding certain educational issues are held and how quickly some congregants *threaten* to leave the congregation.

These crises struck a resonant chord in me. I could vividly remember the bewildering fights that would erupt among the adult members of my parents' synagogue. We children would be waiting for a service to begin when, seemingly without warning, two men would begin shouting at one another at the top of their lungs. These were not personal disputes but very loud disagreements over synagogue practice. One party would often be the *gabbai*—a lay authority—who was perceived as having violated a norm of synagogue life by unfairly overlooking this second person's turn to lead a part of the service. The aggrieved person, who was beside himself with hurt and indignant anger, would express those feelings directly and loudly to the *gabbai*.

As I was puzzling over the mini-crises at Temple Akiba and Temple Hillel, these memories resurfaced. Surely no one I observed objected as loudly or as brusquely as the men I remembered from childhood. But there seemed to be a connection between the behavior I was observing in the present and the intense interpersonal conflict of that Orthodox synagogue during the 1950s. Perhaps this public expression of intense feeling around conflict held some clue to the underlying emotional life of a synagogue.

This hunch led me back to a work that would have a profound influence on this ethnography: Barbara Myerhoff's *Number Our Days*.[27] A wonderfully gifted anthropologist, Myerhoff became interested in studying the process of aging. After fruitlessly pursuing leads in the

Latino community, Myerhoff decided to base her ethno-graphic study of the elderly in an urban day center that served Jews of Eastern European backgrounds. Her portrait of these seniors and their collective life in the center is a gem of ethnographic reporting and analysis. But most significant for my purposes, Myerhoff focuses on the types of mini-crisis that I had observed in the two synagogues.

Myerhoff portrays these elderly Jews as exceedingly disputatious. They constantly fought with one another over causes large and small. They could drive her mad with their repetitive complaints and conflicts. Nothing seemed good enough; no event passed without comment and dispute. Myerhoff, however, did not focus her work on this expressive style itself, but on those central occasions when a dispute transcended the usual bickering—when what might have remained an interpersonal conflict took on new force and threatened to rip apart the communal consensus.

Myerhoff's distinction between interpersonal and communal conflict proved helpful. The loud conflicts I remembered from my childhood were very disturbing to the communal peace. But they did *not* threaten the communal consensus. Congregants may have been divided about who was right or wrong in a given situation, but because they implicitly backed the *gabbai's* right to make these decisions, they were not drawn into the conflict. Perhaps he was in error; but, as with a manager on a 1950s baseball team, it was his call to make.

In this study I was drawn to a different type of dispute that *did* threaten the communal consensus. This type of dispute reflects a fault line in the basic values of the synagogue. Each party to the conflict claims they are right because they are defending a basic value of the synagogue, and each side is correct: it is representing a basic value. The dilemma is that the contemporary synagogue has embraced different and conflicting values. In contrast to the 1950s synagogue, where conflicts took place within a broad consensus over basic values and policies, the contemporary non-Orthodox synagogue lives with a far more complex array of values; it stands for many things at once.

As a result it is more vulnerable to the types of conflict that threaten communal consensus.[28]

Myerhoff offers a frame for understanding this type of conflict. Borrowing from one of her mentors, the anthropologist Victor Turner, she describes these conflicts as "social dramas."

> These are public occasions wherein a significant crisis emerges and is resolved. Usually an orderly sequence of stages occurs: The drama begins when a threat to collective life is perceived. Often this happens when someone in the group violates an important rule or custom. The mechanisms that operate to contain or dispel a conflict fail and the difficulty spreads, drawing in more and more members until it constitutes a real crisis. Some mending, some action that restores order and redresses the violation is called for, and this occurs in the third stage. The last part, the conclusion, achieves an equilibrium and often is accompanied by a realignment of social relationships where dissident factions or individuals are reintegrated into the group. The final stage is often accomplished through symbolic displays of unity or ritual performances that affirm members' widest or most basic beliefs. (pp. 31–32)

Turner and Myerhoff show how an emergent social drama follows several steps towards resolution. These conflicts are not random occurrences but highly structured— even ritualized—dramas. For the participants caught in the throes of the conflict, however, nothing is predictable. They feel their ordered world has been thrown into disarray and that there is no telling what the outcome will be. Their organization is facing a real crisis, and they have a key role to play as actors in the unfolding drama. At a crucial stage the conflict can spread and cause more damage to the communal fabric or move towards redress and healing. That will depend in part on how the actors in the drama play their roles.[29]

Turner's primary interest in describing the social

drama is charting its effects on the social relations of the people caught up in the conflict. While Myerhoff is also interested in this, she pursues another dimension of the social drama that has particular relevance for synagogue life. In some cases social dramas can also function as "definitional-ceremonies." These are conflicts in which:

> No social rearrangements are accomplished, rather redress consists solely of the performance of the group's shared and unquestionable truths. . . . In these dramas they [the group members] develop their collective identity, their interpretation of their world, themselves and their values. (p. 32)

Myerhoff is asserting two points: first, that institutions like synagogues do not simply *have* a collective identity but must *discover* and *develop* their collective identity through action and performance; and second, that values *performed* are more defining than values *declared*.

Myerhoff's two claims are key to my own argument in this book. Synagogues develop reputations among their constituents and within the broader community by the actions they take, including hiring a distinguished rabbi, running an effective school, and building a warm community. The synagogue's reputation—or collective identity— is often challenged by changing realities such as the financial exigencies the synagogue faces or the conflicting demands made by a diverse membership; but before long it is likely that some of the features that define the synagogue's collective identity will be called into question.

When this happens these days, there is *not* likely to be a consensus on how to proceed. Some leaders will suggest that the congregation move in one direction; others will suggest moving in varying directions. Some debate and conflict will ensue. At that moment, Myerhoff suggests, the members of the congregation—whether they think in these terms or not—are doing more than choosing a course of action. They are also choosing to define themselves by articulating for themselves and others what their congregation really values and hence who they are as a collective unit.

Such moments are not easy to negotiate; they are often filled with tensions and the danger of social fragmentation. Yet, they are also potentially productive. For a vital organization cannot afford to simply *have* an identity; its members need to remain active in *defining* and *redefining* that identity.

Redefining can occur through deliberate, rational planning. Committees can meet to develop a mission statement and a vision for the future. Rabbis can lay out the religious and ideological basis for action, and educators can develop programs to educate the membership. But synagogues—like churches and other affiliational groups—are *never* purely rational organizations. Too much of the life of the synagogue is charged with emotion and nonrational attachments. Too much is emotionally and culturally at stake for people. At some point rationality will inevitably give way to drama.[30]

When rational discourse gives way to social drama, a special opportunity opens for the ethnographer to observe the congregation in an act of self-definition. As defining ceremonies, these dramas are enactments of the conflicting stances that make up the congregation's evolving identity. They are the congregation's way of discovering—and the ethnographer's way of observing—the values that most animate the life of the synagogue.

Cultural Performance and Education

> There is a difference between saying "I *am* Jewish" and "I *do* Jewish." You can't just *be* Jewish; because in the United States, you will *be* Christian. (Rabbi Rachel Abeles, Temple Akiba)

Rabbi Abeles' observation returns us to Myerhoff's second point: identity is a matter of actions and performances, not simply of thoughts and feelings. This is not to minimize the role that thoughts and feelings play in the formation of identity but to emphasize that until thoughts and feelings are put into actions—particularly actions that are "cultural performances"—one's identity remains inert. To borrow a phrase, one who simply *feels* Jewish has yet to "come out" as a Jew.

Synagogues are important contexts in American society for performing actions that define one as a Jew. But the cultural performances that synagogues sponsor are often complex and difficult to master. As noted earlier, many Jews feel distant from the rituals and study that make up a large part of the synagogue's religious life. They do not have the familiarity and skill needed to perform the rituals and study in a self-affirming manner.

Synagogue education is often a preparation for assuming an active role in synagogue life. A child or an adult can learn the needed skills for synagogue participation by attending the appropriate educational activities. Both children and adults these days learn much Hebrew and Judaica to prepare for becoming a Bar or Bat Mitzvah. At one's Bar or Bat Mitzvah celebration, the celebrant performs before family, friends, and community the very skills needed to be an active synagogue Jew. The Bar or Bat Mitzvah does not simply proclaim, "Today I am a Jew"; he or she demonstrates the skills acquired for "doing Jewish" within a synagogue context.

If the synagogue's educational agenda is to teach Jews to *do* rather than just *feel* Jewish, then cultural performance has to have a close link to Jewish education. The educational agenda cannot end with teaching knowledge or exploring Jewish values. There need to be the opportunities for youth and adults to put into practice what they learn through the enactment of Jewish cultural and religious performances.

This is a point made vividly by Samuel Heilman in his ethnography of adult Jewish learning, *The People of the Book*. When observing pious Orthodox Jews, whose Jewish identity is established beyond doubt, Heilman found that they delight in the performance of their Jewishness. In gathering to study Torah, they are not simply learning about Jewish law; they are also involved in "enacting, exhibiting, and discovering the meaning of being a Jew."[31] That these advanced Jewish learners continue to discover the meaning of being a Jew is one of the wonders of the cultural performance of Jewish learning.

Borrowing from Heilman's framework for my analysis of synagogue education, I believe that it is a mistake to separate "learning" from "performance"—to isolate the cognitive elements of Jewish learning from the process of enculturation. From what I have seen of school classes and adult study sessions in these two synagogues, when the rhythm is right, there is a fair mix of teaching, learning, and performance going on in any given hour. At a religious service, in which the performance of the ritual is the primary goal, there is still much opportunity for teaching and learning. In a class session on the Bible, where learning the text is the primary goal, there is still ample opportunity for teacher and students to "perform" some aspects of their Jewish identities. I can only echo Heilman in reporting that what makes synagogue life engaging are those moments when these modalities mix. Then children and adults feel that they are being engaged on multiple levels: their minds are being stretched, their skills are on display, and their hearts are stirred.

As a participant-observer in the educational sessions of these synagogues, I would look beyond the story line of the lesson—beyond what was being talked about—to try to discern the dynamics of the cultural performance. I wanted to feel the drama of the interaction—to know what was going on for the participants. At times very little was going on besides their coping with the demands of classroom life; but on some occasions, I could catch a rhythm of excitement that animated their participation.

To illustrate my interest in Jewish learning as cultural performance, I will briefly summarize a family education session at Temple Akiba that will be discussed more fully in Chapter 2. The topic of this session was "Death in the Family"—a topic that fit into the sixth-grade curriculum on the Jewish life cycle. Present at this Sunday morning session were the sixth graders, many of their parents, and their teachers.

In one corner of this family education event, I sat with a group of parents and children who were discussing with the teacher the Jewish ways of mourning. The parents and children came with fragmentary knowledge of what they had seen and heard about Jewish mourning rituals. As a group they pieced together their impressions to create a clearer picture than they had before. The discussion was animated by recollection, curiosity, and the wish to know more.

In the midst of the discussion, one mother slipped in a mention of her husband's recent death. She wanted the others to know that the rabbis had been very helpful to her and that performing the rituals of mourning were comforting "when you're overwhelmed and don't know what to do."

At this moment in the session I realized far more was going on than a simple review of the rituals of mourning. Most of the parents in this session did not know each other well. They only rarely got together as a group. Yet as they and the children engaged in the discussion, a group was forming. I could feel it myself as I sat with them. What united the group was some knowledge of these Jewish rituals as well as a great curiosity about them. Why rend one's garment after hearing of the death? Why cover the mirrors or wear slippers during the *shivah* period? In asking these questions, the parents and children shared a common concern and voiced a common sense of mystery about these rituals.

When the mother unexpectedly shared her deeply personal experiences, I suddenly felt close to tears. What courage it took to speak of her husband's death with her child sitting next to her. What composure she had to speak those words without crying or asking for sympathy. What a comfort it was for the group to know that with the rabbis' help, these rituals worked to soothe this family's shock at a time of acute loss.

As this small group discussion ended, I thought: here are parents and children learning together on many levels. One level was the cognitive—the information and understanding gained about these rituals. But beyond learning information, the parents and children, by watching and listening to one another, were participating together in a cultural performance. Through this performance, they were expressing a wish: that when they too die, they want to be buried and mourned as Jews. This yearning—which the adults shared with their children—added greatly to the significance of the lesson on mourning rituals.

Sitting with these parents and children as they came alive with a heightened level of interest and engagement, I felt as if an electrical current were running through this group. I could feel the current running through me as well, leading me to wonder: What makes this educational moment so alive?

There could be many answers to this question. The one I am focusing on here has to do with cultural performance. As with the Orthodox men who became enraptured with their study of Talmud, these participants in a temple family educational session "took off" with this material to go beyond a level of intellectual interest to an engagement with their own mortality and sense of finitude. They discovered that aspect of Jewish education that addresses not only the here and now, but also the more ultimate concern: Who will take care of me and my loved ones when death appears at the family's door?

Being a participant-observer this year taught me about the many ways that people in synagogues learn about themselves as Jews and about the traditions of Judaism. Many of those lessons come through the more conventional modes of instructions: teaching, sermonizing, and discussing. But some lessons come through the less well understood means of cultural performances and social dramas. I focus in this book more on the latter kind of lesson than on the former with the hope of exploring the full range of ways that synagogues educate their members. If educators, rabbis, and parents can better recognize and understand the rhythms of cultural performance and social drama, they may become more aware of the power inherent in religious education. If awareness is a step towards responsible implementation, perhaps we may look forward to programs of religious education that are as dramatically engaging as they are cognitively instructive.

Chapter 2
Educating the Adults

In studying the educating synagogue, where does one begin? An observer who follows the numbers will be drawn to the religious school, where the heaviest flow of traffic leads. In any given week during the school year, the number of children and parents who enter the synagogue and head for the school far exceeds those who enter for other reasons. One might even observe that on Sunday mornings, when kindergarten through seventh grade are in session and there are special programs for family education, the parking lot is filled to capacity in a way that is rare on Shabbat and most Jewish holidays (with the clear exception of the High Holidays).

Yet, I believe it would be a serious mistake to follow the numbers. Children in the religious school do not set the agenda for Jewish education in the synagogue. Nor for the most part do their teachers. Rather, that agenda gets set between the rabbis and the adult congregants. An observer has to attend the worship services, the adult and family education sessions, and the meetings of key groups and committees to get a feeling for the Jewish educational agenda of the synagogue.

But what is meant by the "educational agenda of the synagogue?" Neither the board of directors nor any other decision-making body within a synagogue gets together with the rabbis to set an official educational agenda. In most cases, there is nothing in writing that defines this agenda. But there is, I am claiming, an observable agenda—one that permeates the educating synagogue and distinguishes a given synagogue from the others in the area. I would call this agenda the "distinctive Torah" taught at that synagogue.

"Distinctive Torah" is the style of approach to the study and celebration of Judaism that characterizes a given synagogue. In some instances, that "Torah" is set by a charismatic rabbi. In other instances, a synagogue sets its style over time and seeks professionals—a rabbi, a cantor, and an educator—whose teachings fit that style. At times a synagogue has an established style and hires a new rabbi who brings a new "Torah." That rabbi may then struggle to change the Jewish approach of that synagogue to reflect more closely the "Torah" he has come to teach. Such was the case, as we will see, at Temple Akiba.

The "distinctive Torah" will usually fall within the broad parameters of the synagogue's denomination. An Orthodox synagogue will expect its rabbi to teach Torah in a way that can be recognized as Orthodox. Yet, as Heilman has clearly shown, within flourishing Orthodox communities the Torah that is taught is far from one-dimensional. Orthodox rabbis who share many doctrinal beliefs in common may still develop distinctively different approaches to teaching Torah. And it is those individual differences that their followers seem to cherish.[1]

The same can be said for the rabbis in the Reform movement. They teach Torah in a way that is recognizable as fitting within the Reform movement. Surely Reform rabbis share many similar beliefs, but significant differences are noticeable among them. Rabbi Davidman, at Temple Akiba, stresses the centrality of studying the classical texts of Judaism—preferably in the Hebrew—although many of his colleagues in other synagogues focus their teaching on more contemporary theological problems. Learning Judaism from one rabbi is an intellectually and emotionally different experience from learning from any other rabbi.

Were these different approaches simply the individual preferences of the rabbis, they would be interesting to note but not highly relevant to this study. When I arrived to study Temple Akiba, Rabbi Davidman had been in his post as senior rabbi for over a decade. During this time, he had played a very active role as an educational leader within the synagogue, he had helped hire the educational director and worked closely with him, and he had taught and worked closely with the lay leadership of the synagogue. His influence—indeed his "distinctive Torah"—had become a collective mandate. Yes, that "Torah" could and would be challenged by segments of the congregation. In my observation, however, it set the educational agenda for this synagogue and its school.

In a metropolitan area with a sizable Jewish population and a large number of synagogues, it makes pragmatic as well as religious sense for a temple to develop a distinctive educational approach. While location and denomination can play important roles in Jews' choices of which synagogue to join, educational approach can also be an important factor. Most new members are parents with children of school or preschool age. In many cases they want to know the quality of education offered by the synagogue. If, as I am claiming, the quality of the synagogue school is a reflection of the educational agenda that permeates the congregation, a synagogue with a "distinctive Torah" to teach will have an advantage over those with weaker agendas.

How the Temple Akiba rabbis—Norman Davidman, Don Marcus, and Rachel Abeles—work with the adult members to establish the educational agenda for this synagogue is a key issue. As senior rabbi, Norman clearly sets the tone. But Don had been his rabbinic partner for many years and plays a key role in setting the educational agenda. Rachel, in her first year at Temple Akiba, was learning their approach. We will observe Rabbi Davidman teaching Torah study for adults, Rabbi Abeles leading a *seliḥot* study service, and Rabbi Marcus teaching at a family education event. We will place those individual portraits in a larger context by showing how the "distinctive Torah" the rabbis teach stands in some tension with the history of this once classically Reform congregation.

Shabbat Morning

On a Shabbat morning in February Rabbi Marcus was walking down Beech Avenue on his way to Temple Akiba. Clad in an open coat and a brown suit, Rabbi Marcus seemed absorbed, and his handsome face wore the signs of fatigue. When we met at the corner of Maple Street, he began telling me of the trip to Israel he had taken during the school break. Immersed in conversation, we crossed the small bridge over the river that divides suburb from city and leads to the temple on the city side.

As the temple educator, Rabbi Marcus is in charge of all the educational activities—especially the religious school, which serves children in kindergarten through twelfth grade. As one of the three rabbis, he also takes his turn leading the adult Torah study group that meets each Saturday morning for an hour before the main Shabbat service begins. As we entered the temple building, I assumed this was Don's turn to lead Torah study. He ducked into the school office, and I continued down the corridor to the lounge. Once seated, I was surprised to see Rabbi Davidman, the senior rabbi, enter in his brisk pace and move to the head of the table. Thinking that on returning from Israel, Rabbi Marcus could use a rest, Rabbi Davidman had prepared in his stead.

There is a special chemistry between Rabbi Davidman and this group of Torah students. Most of the thirty members—some of whom are well into their seventies and eighties—have been around the temple longer than he and can remember an earlier era in which this style of close textual study was not yet the norm. Most are vibrantly curious about Judaism and drink in Norman's vast knowledge of Bible and commentaries. Most grew up in schools and synagogues in which the teachers and rabbis were respected as authorities—and Rabbi Davidman is certainly authoritative in his teaching style. Having completed a doctorate in Judaica while serving a former congregation, Rabbi Davidman, Temple Akiba's senior rabbi is a scholar as well as a pastor.

Meeting on a regular weekly basis, the Torah study group has become one of the mini-communities within this large congregation. Many of its members come at 9:00 A.M. and conduct their own early-morning service before study commences. Few stay for the 10:30 service in the main sanctuary. Instead, they seem happy to have the rabbis mainly for the purpose of study, which in Temple Akiba often is a more intimate experience than worship in the large, beautiful but impersonal main sanctuary.

At Temple Akiba it is no accident that Rabbi Marcus also takes his turn in teaching the adults. Running the religious school and the youth groups are his main responsibilities, but he sees educating the adults as an important part of his mission. For there is not one "Torah" for the adults and another for the children. Rather, Rabbis Davidman and Marcus have a singular approach to teaching Judaism that is implemented differently in adult study and in the religious school. To understand how Rabbi Marcus thinks about educating the children, we first have to understand how Torah is presented to the adults.

Torah Study

On each Shabbat a different Torah portion is studied. This week's was *Tetzaveh* (Exodus 27:20–30:10), a rather unexciting recitation of the rituals associated with the Tabernacle in the desert. Rabbi Davidman announced that this time they would not be studying the biblical text itself—their usual practice—but the midrash on the text. He handed out copies of selections from Exodus Rabbah[2] and explained that these rabbinic commentaries on Exodus had been collected and edited late in the rabbinic period.

Faced with a biblical text—like *Tetzaveh*—that lacks the narrative charm of Genesis or the legal poignancy of Deuteronomy, a rabbi has many pedagogic choices. The rabbi may turn historian and deal with the history of the period, turn moralist and deal with the moral import, or turn contemporary commentator and jump off from the text to the business of living in today's world. Most rabbis know the tricks of this trade and have taken these paths on weeks like this.

Rabbi Davidman made another choice: to introduce the midrashic text and study it in detail. Were that text itself more accessible than the biblical text, or were it to contain a clear and relevant message, Rabbi Davidman's choice would make apparent sense. But that is not the case.

The midrashic text was more complex and did not yield any obvious moral lesson. That leaves us to wonder why he made this choice. What does his choice signify?

This midrashic text, which the group took turns reading out loud, quotes a verse from the Torah and then explains its metaphoric meanings, which often depart sharply from its plain meaning. The focus of this midrashic text is on the first verse of Exodus, 27:20: "And thou shalt command the children of Israel that they bring unto thee pure olive oil beaten for the light to cause a lamp to burn continually." The midrash draws attention to the olive tree and the olive that is beaten to produce its oil.

> As the olive is brought down from the tree and beaten . . . and stones are bought for further pressing . . . so it is for Israel . . . who are beaten by heathens, imprisoned and bound in chains . . . until at last Israel repent and God answers them.

Rabbi Davidman noted that the midrash's focus on beating the olive is telling, for that is not at the center of the Torah verse. Yet, that choice reflects how the rabbis saw the place of the people Israel in their times and the relationship between the people and their God.

While the members of the study group took turns reading this difficult text, I wondered what sense they were making of its images. Were they taken aback by the suggestion that Israel is beaten—as one would beat an olive—until they repent? But if anyone was taken aback, I did not hear any evidence of it. Many questions were asked, but all were requests for clarification of how to read the text. The group was hard at work deciphering the midrash.

As a volunteer was about to read the second midrash, Rabbi Davidman interposed, "You won't like this one as much." Calling this midrash "a sermon on intermarriage," he suggested that intermarriage must have been an issue even in those days. The midrash opens by asking how Israel can be compared to an olive tree: "All liquids commingle with one another, but oil refuses to do so and stays separate. So Israel does not mingle with the heathen."

I thought, if one thing has changed with time, it is Israel's refusal to "mingle with the heathen." But the group was silent on this issue. They seemed pleased with themselves for having read and decoded this second midrash. The reading of the third midrash drew a different reaction, however.

> As olive oil floats on top, even after it has been mixed with every kind of liquid in the world . . . so it is with Israel who, as long as they perform the will of God, stand higher than the heathen.

Perhaps the force of this formulation shook the group loose, for as soon as the reading was completed, Bruce's hand shot up. "Where does the universal message come in?" In reviewing the midrash's images, Bruce concludes, "This is clearly particularistic."

Steve added a second question: "If Israel stands higher than the heathen, how can someone who converts [to Judaism] be included in this? If the converted is not biologically descended, can he be included?"

Even before the rabbi responded, I heard an unspoken question behind their inquiries. Temple Akiba is a congregation with a proud history of rabbis who put special emphasis in their Torah teaching on the universal message in Judaism. Never would they have spoken of Jews as "oil [that] floats on top" or of Israel as "higher than the heathen." The emphasis would have been on "being a light to the nations" but not a light "above the nations." Perhaps Bruce and Steve were asking Rabbi Davidman how these provocative midrashic formulations square with the past Torah taught at this synagogue.

But Rabbi Davidman chose to address the direct and not the unspoken questions. He told Bruce that he was right to characterize this midrash as having a particularistic message but that there are earlier midrashic commentaries on Exodus that do have a more universal message.[3] He told Steve that Maimonides, the great medieval sage, addressed his question and declared that one who converts becomes a part of the elect.[4] When Steve countered that this response "is not rational," Rabbi Davidman laughed, "No, it's not rational. But who said these things need be rational?"

The rest of the hour was spent puzzling over the next midrash, which discusses the light given off by the olive oil and, by analogy, the divine light. The session came to a close at 10:30, when Rabbi Davidman dashed off to the large Shabbat service and left the men and women to wrap up final thoughts among themselves.

I was chatting with some of the group members whom I previously knew, when Bruce came over and introduced himself. A doctor at a university hospital, he said he comes to study in search of "a deeper element in Judaism than is available through the Reform Jewish liturgy." Shaken by the degree of human pain he encounters in the hospital, he is looking for a religious response. Bruce found meaning in the midrash, especially in the image of God as responding to Israel in its moments of distress.

Bruce's search for a "deeper element in Judaism than is available in the Reform Jewish liturgy" served as a clue to what Rabbi Davidman's teaching meant in this context. For studying these midrashic texts takes this group well beyond the parameters of the liberal religious language that forms the backbone of Reform liturgy. This study takes them to a metaphoric plane on which Israel suffers for its sins and God sends the divine light only after a painful process of purification. Bruce was gaining access to core Jewish religious language that he would not hear in the Temple Akiba sanctuary, where reference to God tends to be careful and correct.

This study group in the lounge is not an Orthodox branch of Temple Akiba. The same rabbi who teaches these texts co-leads the worship service in the sanctuary and sees the two activities as complementary. One hour he takes some of his most committed members on an exploration of rabbinic texts that he finds exhilarating—if, at times, problematic. The next hour he leads families of Bar and Bat Mitzvah children through a prayer service that, for all its lack of daring religious images, serves their ritual needs quite well.

In Rabbi Davidman's view, worship and study are interrelated aspects of one larger vision of synagogue life. They are designed to complement and reinforce one another and to offer congregants diverse ways of enacting their Judaism. For in a synagogue as large and diverse as Temple Akiba, there may be a unified approach to Jewish education, but there cannot be a single way of studying or praying. There need to be multiple pathways so that congregants with very different levels of commitment to Judaism can grow in their Judaism while still remaining members of a single congregation. The study group in the lounge represents the advanced adult learners in this congregation who want more depth than is commonly available in the large services and lectures. They want what the rabbis have to offer in textual study. They are prepared to more directly learn the "distinctive Torah" of Temple Akiba.

A Distinctive Torah

One study session alone can provide only a few clues to the "distinctive Torah" taught at Temple Akiba. But looking at this session in the context of the many times I observed Rabbi Davidman's teaching and spoke with him about his teaching suggests there is a clear pattern at work: Rabbi Davidman has a "distinctive Torah" that he teaches. In this session his "distinctive Torah" was evident in his decision to move beyond the biblical text to a study of the midrash. The decision signals that such a move is permissible, and even desirable, within the rules for Torah study.

To understand this signal, one must step back and consider the context for this decision. The study of Torah is so central to the practice of Judaism that every movement within Judaism has evolved rules or norms for how Torah study should be conducted. These rules will indicate how broadly "Torah" is to be defined: what the canon of Torah is, and within that canon, what are the essential texts to be studied and how those texts are best studied by learners at different levels of competence. Thus for traditional Eastern European Jewry there was a basic "curriculum" for the unlearned men on Shabbat, another curriculum for the learned graduates of the yeshivah, and yet another for the women who were taught from a Yiddish, rather than a Hebrew, text.

When the children and grandchildren of those Jews came to North America, they tried to perpetuate the European curricula, but soon discovered the old ways would not hold in the new world. Linguistic competencies shifted. More essentially, the definition of who is an educated person dramatically shifted. With public education widely available to American Jews in a way unthinkable in Eastern Europe, Jews quickly adopted the norm that fluency in English and in the intellectual currents of Western civilization was the mark of the educated.

When the first rabbinical school on this continent was opened over a hundred years ago, its founders did not call the institution a yeshivah, but a college. The opening of Hebrew Union College signaled that being an American rabbi meant having a college education—a norm that would be adopted by all denominations but the ultra-Orthodox.[5] At Hebrew Union College, *Torah* would be translated as *Bible,* and *Bible* would mean what the Christians called the Old Testament. More significantly Jews would learn from liberal Protestants that in the twentieth century an educated person does not study Bible as the word of God given on Mount Sinai and interpreted faithfully by the rabbis of the Talmud. Rather, an educated person studies Bible in historical terms, as an ancient religious text that is best interpreted against its ancient Near Eastern background. How the rabbis of another historical era—that is, the talmudic or medieval era—commented on the Torah is of interest but is rarely the definitive interpretation.[6]

A rabbi trained to read Torah this way at either Hebrew Union College (which trains Reform rabbis) or the Jewish Theological Seminary (which trains Conservative rabbis) would have to create a new curriculum to engage congregants in Torah study. The approach would be to encourage learners to take the Torah seriously but not literally. The curriculum would teach learners to distinguish the essential lessons of Torah from those other aspects of biblical legislation or morality that might be seen as "remnants of an ancient age." Undoubtedly the different religious movements and rabbis within those movements created their own distinctive language for teaching Torah, but there were certain rules or norms for teaching Torah that most knew and followed.[7]

Classical Reform Judaism, as practiced at Temple Akiba for many decades of this century, went quite far in stripping Torah down to its essentials. At some points there was little emphasis placed on the Hebrew text of Torah, little value seen in studying any rabbinic commentary; most emphasis was placed on the Prophets and on prophetic Judaism.[8] Even when more Hebrew and broader Torah study were reintroduced into the curriculum—which will be discussed in the coming chapters—there was still little reliance on rabbinic sources, except when a famous rabbinic statement seemed especially apt for contemporary times. The main thrust of the Torah curriculum—whether for adults or for children—was to show that Judaism is a religion for modern times that has much to teach people today about living the good life in contemporary society.

With this approach to Torah study there is no point in teaching the midrash on the olive tree. Why introduce images of God and Israel that are so foreign to modern consciousness? What can a modern Jew possibly learn from this rabbinic text other than about the suffering that Jews experienced in the Roman Empire after the destruction of the Temple? With the precious few minutes that are available for Torah study, how can this pedagogic choice be justified?

Rabbi Davidman does not justify his decision; he simply makes it. But in considering why this study group accepts his decision—why, in fact, it gets engrossed in following the intricate moves of the midrashic author—I realize that previous to this session their rabbi has already introduced them to a new curriculum. They already understand that the rules for Torah study have changed at Temple Akiba and that this particular move makes sense in the context of a new curriculum that Rabbi Davidman has introduced.

Essential to the new curriculum is that although Norman never asks his students to give up their modern consciousness or their liberal orientation, he takes them on a journey into the heartland of classical rabbinic thought. There they encounter terms that are unfamiliar, ideas that are foreign to their daily assumptions, and images that run counter to the teachings of modern, liberal religion. He leads them beyond the cognitive borders of the familiar and the comfortable—not to abandon their own faith positions, but to open themselves to the less rational and more spiritual aspects of classical Jewish thought.

In leading these adult learners, Norman often intersperses his explanation of the text with Hebrew terms that he does not translate. For example, he consistently refers to the author of the text as the *ba'al hamidrash*—the master of the midrash. That is a common Hebrew phrase, but not familiar to most Americans Jews. I was not sure that most of the participants could translate the term, but from the context, they seemed to grasp its meaning. That no one asked for a translation for this or any other of the Hebrew terms used suggested that Norman has established that a certain level of Hebrew comprehension is expected for those who would undertake this journey.

At an earlier session of this group, when Norman was using a Hebrew phrase he did not translate, he noticed a puzzled look on the face of one of the students. "You don't seem happy," he said to the woman. "I'm happy—happy in my ignorance," she replied. "No," the rabbi insisted, "that was in a past age. Now we are no longer happy in our ignorance."

This phrase—"we are no longer happy in our ignorance"—is key to Norman's approach. The "we" refers to the members of this temple who for most of this century have prided themselves on their modern, rational approach to Judaism. But that approach comes with a cost: a constricted focus on a narrow band of Jewish texts and concepts that seem to fit the assumptions of modernity. It was those texts that were studied, primarily in translation. In reaction to that tendency, Norman is widening the scope of the traditional Jewish texts and concepts that are

encountered in the study sessions and classes of this synagogue. He is saying, in effect, Let us modern Jews make
our religious choices not from ignorance, but from a fuller
understanding of Jewish tradition.

By leading his congregants into the midrashic discourse, Norman is also engaging them in a different type
of learning from that once typical in this synagogue. This is
not a frontal teaching format in which the rabbi unpacks
the text, but an interactive exercise in encountering the
unfamiliar and rendering it more intelligible bit by bit.
This Torah study is reminiscent of Heilman's descriptions
of study circles in Jerusalem in which Orthodox Jewish
men regularly meet together to study Talmud.

> Listening to himself and his fellows bring to life
> the voice of the Talmud, . . . the participant not only
> learns what the texts have to say; he also has a
> chance *to say it himself, to reenact and react to it.* . . . By
> so doing, he publicly reflects, communicates, perpet-
> uates, and develops the pattern of meanings and
> inherited conceptions that define traditional Jewish
> culture. In this sense, *lernen* may be termed a *cultural
> performance.* (p.61)

The participants in Temple Akiba's Torah study also
are "culturally performing" traditional Jewish study. Their
line-by-line struggle with the midrashic text—albeit in
translation—brings them into a direct encounter with the
midrashic form of exegesis. Yet, as modern liberal Jews,
they do not have the same relationship to this text as do
the Orthodox. If the Orthodox men in Heilman's study are
reflecting, communicating, and perpetuating a traditional
Jewish culture which they believe they have received from
their fathers and forefathers, the Temple Akiba members
are reflecting and communicating a nontraditional culture
of American Judaism. Not only were they not taught by
their parents to study these texts, they were also not
encouraged in previous generations by their own rabbis to
study in this fashion.

This cultural discontinuity does not diminish their cultural performance, but it does alter it. Rabbi Davidman is breaking new ground with them. This traditional rabbinic exegesis remains for them—as for most non-Orthodox American Jews—a novelty. It fascinates but also confuses. How does it relate to all that they have been taught by their earlier rabbis about Judaism as a modern religion? When Bruce asked about the universal message and Steve about the authority of rationalism, they were asking about articles of faith that were not long ago preached from the pulpit of this temple.

This Torah study session reflects a change in synagogue culture towards greater acceptance of and comfort with traditional forms of Jewish activity. The Reform movement, in parallel with similar developments in the Conservative, Reconstructionist, and Orthodox movements, has been moving, over the past two decades, toward the reincorporation of elements of Jewish tradition that were either rejected or not emphasized in earlier decades of this century.[9] At Temple Akiba this includes not only learning a new approach to Torah study, but also implementing major ritual and liturgical changes that will be described.

These members of Temple Akiba—like most members of American synagogues—are participants in a religious culture that undergoes constant change in its beliefs and practices. Rabbi Davidman has called for a reconsideration of many of the major tenets of Judaism as practiced at Temple Akiba. The innovations in teaching that were evident in this Torah study group are not an isolated phenomenon. They are of a piece with the religious leadership that Rabbis Davidman and Marcus have exercised since their arrival at Temple Akiba.

To understand the ways this synagogue educates its members, we must consider these rabbis' larger vision of synagogue life. What they teach—and how they teach—is an outgrowth of their vision of "the good synagogue." They came to Temple Akiba with a mission to revitalize an aging congregation, and they view education as a major tool in their plans for revitalization. Seeing this larger picture will allow us to place what we have seen in one Torah study group in a larger context.

Revitalizing an Aging Congregation

Ten years after their arrival at Temple Akiba, Rabbis Davidman and Marcus prepared a joint autobiographic statement that they presented as part of a scholar-in-residence weekend on the role of the rabbi and function of the synagogue. Rabbi Marcus shared the transcript of this talk with me. It is a remarkable document for what it reveals about the rabbis' vision of their work.

Vision is no small part of leadership. To understand the culture of Temple Akiba requires first apprehending the program set forth by the rabbis and then the real-life constraints operating in the organization. The picture the rabbis painted in this talk is consistent with what they presented to me in private interviews and what I heard each present in other public contexts. It is the official version of their work together, "a sacred story, a personal myth which takes up the ultimate eschatological questions, 'What has it all meant?' 'Why was I here?'"[10] The rabbis continually hold up this sacred story as a way of communicating where the congregation has been moving, why it is moving in that direction, and what still needs to be accomplished to complete the journey.

Their story begins before their coming to Temple Akiba. In the early 1970s Norman was a young rabbi in a small congregation in another city, and Don was a rabbinical student still unsure of his career path. Norman was looking for a rabbinic intern and recruited Don to join him:

> As soon as Simḥat Torah was over, I led a group of members on a three-week trip to Israel. Don was in charge of the temple, the Davidman quick-method to become a rabbi. In my absence Don not only navigated the shoals of temple life, he also developed a deep and abiding friendship with Lucy and my young sons.

Working with Norman gave Don a chance to sort out his doubts.

We sat one night conversing, during which I expressed my doubts about myself and the rabbinate. How can I possibly become a rabbi when I haven't figured out what I believe about God? Norman quoted Buber and spoke about the primary importance of interpersonal human relations. He told me that I had plenty of time to figure out the rest. In that moment I was sure that my intuitive decision had been correct.

After working together, the two men remained close friends as Don completed his rabbinic training, got married, and served in his first rabbinic position, as an assistant in a large congregation. Norman happily remained in his small congregation while he was raising young children, building the congregation, pursuing a doctorate, and becoming involved in an experimental seminary.

The call to consider the senior position at Temple Akiba came as a surprise to Norman. A recent synagogue president, a strong supporter of his, filled in her version of what happened.

The search committee for the new rabbi knew they did not want another "cathedral rabbi." Yet that was who was being sent as candidates. The president was interested in Rabbi Norman Davidman from a small congregation in another city. He went to see him in action and came back with the recommendation that Davidman be seriously considered. I'm not sure the board knew what they were getting in selecting Davidman, but they hired him.

A cathedral rabbi is an orator who can fill a cathedral-size sanctuary with the fullness of his or her message. It is a rabbi for the High Holidays who can preach to an impressive crowd and move them through sheer rhetorical power. Temple Akiba had rabbis who could fill that bill and more. But now the leadership was looking for another, gentler model of rabbi who could touch people more in the everyday realm, who could attract a next generation less moved by rhetoric and more by the sincerity of personal relationships. Perhaps that is what the board saw in Norman Davidman.

But, as Don relates about a visit they had before Norman's interview, Norman was not so sure he wanted this position.

> In a remarkable reversal of roles I became the counselor trying to sift and sort the doubts and uncertainties that he expressed. "Why would they choose me?" he asked. "But what do you want?" I responded. To our mutual surprise, Norman admitted that he was honestly interested in the position. I remember putting him on the plane with the words, "Every once in a while in this racket the right thing happens for the right person."

After arriving at Temple Akiba in 1978, Norman discovered that the assistant rabbi was completing his contract and was offered a senior position in another city. Norman knew whom he wanted to fill this position, and by summer he had brought the Marcuses to town.

Together they described their initial assessment of the temple:

> We found a congregation with a distinguished history, proud of its past, its accomplishments and its contributions to Reform Judaism. It was a temple which took pride in a distinguished rabbinate. . . . [I]t was easy to acknowledge our indebtedness to the work of our predecessors. We encountered lay leaders who communicated their commitment to a tradition of service and a dedication to the continuity of the temple. . . . We were impressed that the elders of the temple understood the myriad of changes that were taking place within the local community and on the broader American Jewish scene.

But they did remain with a question: Given the temple's long and proud history, would its reputation for conservatism inhibit the opportunity for change? Their conclusion was optimistic. "We discovered an open-minded conservatism which expressed itself in a reverence for the best of the past coupled with a willingness to permit us to risk their future."

What goes unstated here, and requires a knowledge of the temple's history to appreciate, was that the vision of a personal Judaism that these rabbis were presenting was sufficiently at odds with the formal, almost impersonal tendencies of this historic temple to leave even the rabbis wondering if the congregation had the inner flexibility to accommodate to the rabbis' prescription for its future. This, however, was by no means the first time in its history that Temple Akiba faced the challenge of adjusting to a new rabbi with a new vision.

The Temple's History

Temple Akiba's history extends back to the nineteenth century, when a small group of Jewish immigrants from Germany decided to begin their own synagogue rather than continue praying with fellow Jews from Eastern Europe. Their small synagogue began as a traditional place of worship, with Hebrew liturgy, separate seating, and conversation in German. Only after a period of financial gain and acculturation to American life did the members hire a rabbi to modernize their style of worship. The earliest reforms included the introduction of mixed seating, an organ and choir, and a new English-Hebrew prayer book. Those changes occasioned a storm of protest and resignations; but those who remained, and the second generation who joined, set out on a program of radical reform. By the early twentieth century, the now-prosperous German-Jewish congregation had discarded all distinctive religious garb and dietary habits, removed much of the Hebrew liturgy, and replaced it with more inspirational readings stressing the prophetic tradition in Judaism and the messianic hope for universal justice, equality, and peace. They moved their primary weekly service from Saturday to Sunday and opened that service to many non-Jews. At the center of the service was the long sermon—actually a lecture—offered by their erudite, articulate, and very liberal rabbi.[11]

By the second decade of this century, the radical Reform practices of their rabbi came to feel too extreme, and when the rabbi left, the lay leaders hired a more classically Reform rabbi.[12] He introduced a series of changes in the congregation that brought Temple Akiba more into the mainstream of Reform Judaism. These included restoring the Saturday service and keeping the Sunday service, beginning a serious Sunday school for religious instruction, sponsoring a congregational seder, and starting a sisterhood and brotherhood as well as a Jewish theater group. In the 1920s the temple experienced a period of growth, and for the first time large numbers of Jews from Eastern European backgrounds joined as members. With the introduction of radio, the rabbi's Sunday sermons were broadcast and became popular with both Jews and non-Jews.

The 1929 crash and the depression of the 1930s hit the temple hard. Many of the more recent members left, and the temple found it difficult to finance the expansions undertaken in the 1920s. Furthermore, the optimistic, rationalist, universalistic theology that the rabbi continued to preach seemed vastly out of step with the very worrisome rise of Nazism in Germany and the anti-Semitism around the world and in this country. The classical Reform opposition to Zionism, which in the 1920s may have made sense to prosperous American Jews, seemed unhelpful to Jews who in the 1930s were beginning to worry seriously about the well-being of their people in Europe.[13]

When the rabbi retired in the late 1930s, a young, dynamic rabbi was appointed who initiated the next series of changes for the temple. These included abolishing Sunday services and replacing them with late Friday night services, reintroducing the Bar Mitzvah celebration on Saturday morning, including more Hebrew and traditional rituals in services, and greatly expanding the Jewish curriculum of the school. The new rabbi brought in a new theological stance and expressed openly his support for Zionist aspirations for a Jewish homeland. He was a pioneer in introducing pastoral counseling in the congregation and was able to be of comfort to his congregation as they lived through the very dark days of the war and destruction of European Jewry. He continued and expanded the use of radio broadcasts and made a name for himself and his congregation as his prominence grew through the 1940s.

The post–World War II period was another era of expansion for the temple. As the German-Jewish hold on power decreased and more descendants of Eastern European Jews joined the temple, membership increased. The success of the religious school drew very large numbers of children, and religious school held sessions on both Saturdays and Sundays. When a new rabbi was appointed in the mid-1950s, he continued his predecessor's strong Zionist stance and his reincorporation of traditional Jewish ceremonies. In addition, his prophetic activism in confronting the ills that beset American society made him and his congregation leaders in the civil rights and peace movements of the 1960s.

The 1970s were a more difficult time. The baby boom was over, and the pool of children for the school began to shrink. The urban location of the temple made it less attractive to an increasingly suburban Jewish population. The bulk of the membership was aging, and the temple was not doing well in attracting younger members. It had a reputation for being big, impersonal, and uninviting. Even though it had moved away from being a German-dominated, classical Reform temple, it still had that reputation. Its proud history was working against Temple Akiba when in 1978 Rabbis Davidman and Marcus undertook the challenge of leadership.

Creating a Synagogue Community

In making their assessment of Temple Akiba, the rabbis' primary concern was, would it "be possible to create a community of a large, diverse, aging, urban congregation?" Could this synagogue, with all its history and resources, "be transformed into a vital center for communal Jewish living?"

The terms *community* and *center* are central to the rabbis' vision. At a talk that I heard Norman deliver at a local university, he told of having met the philosopher Martin Buber when he was a rabbinical student in Jerusalem: "In those meetings Buber reiterated that the key to a spiritual life and creating a community was a living center. Later I understood what that meant for my life."

A living center stands at the metaphorical heart of a community and inspires members of the community to ethical and religious action. In congregational life, when a living center draws people to join in mutual commitment to achieve common spiritual goals, a community grows around these people's involvement. Without such a center, membership in the synagogue means little more than an affiliation with another Jewish organization.

In setting out to create community at Temple Akiba, Norman and Don delineated the three areas in which they wished to work: "(1) The need to humanize this formidable and formal institution; (2) developing an extensive program of education; and (3) developing an innovative and participatory approach to the worship experience."

In the rabbis' view, humanizing the institution proceeds along two simultaneous paths: drawing people into the center and moving them out to shared involvement in the world. The rabbis were aware that there are many Jews who perceive themselves to be marginal to the Jewish community because they are not living in a traditional lifestyle; they may be single, widowed, or divorced, married to a non-Jew, or gay or lesbian.

These marginal Jews imagine synagogues to be the province of the straight-and-narrow Jews, and in the case of Temple Akiba, the well-heeled, well-educated Jews. That perception itself becomes self-sealing: as fewer and fewer Jews see themselves as fitting the definition of the Jewish mainstream, the circle of synagogue members in fact grows smaller. Rabbis Davidman and Marcus quickly grasped that this perception needed to be reversed; they realized that at the core of their efforts to humanize the temple stood the question of who belongs here.

> We believe it is incumbent on the modern syna-
> gogue to reach out and embrace the diverse con-
> stituent elements of the community . . . to reach out
> and touch individual lives with the clear message
> that there is room in this house. . . . [T]hey are a part
> of this family.

"Reach out," "embrace," and "touch" are tactile words
that convey the wish for contact. The rabbis were stating
their readiness to embrace the individuals on the margins
as "a part of [the temple] family."

To translate this into action, the rabbis launched a
series of outreach programs, each designed to involve a
different population on the margins of the Jewish community. These populations included the intermarried and
potential converts; various types of families, but especially
single parents and their children; the elderly; gay and lesbian Jews; and Soviet Jews arriving as new Americans. In
some cases Temple Akiba was pioneering in its efforts; in
others, it was joining with the broader synagogue and
Jewish federation movements. In all cases there was a conscious effort to expand the definition of who belonged to
this synagogue community.

Along with drawing these constituencies into the temple, the rabbis extended the reach of the synagogue out
into the broader world. Giving special emphasis to its role
as an urban congregation, the rabbis wanted to reach out
and help the needy in the area. This began with the elderly.
A Caring Committee was established whose first function
was to arrange for members to pay friendly visits to others
who were old, frail, and shut-ins. Temple Akiba has a substantial percentage of members who are elderly. While
many are healthy, others are not and cannot come to the
temple. When they are ill and hospitalized, they are visited
by the clergy. But the committee took on the mitzvah of
visiting those who are at home and in need of company.

The temple has a social action committee, which has
been active in collecting food and shelter for local shelters.
At some point in the 1980s that involvement expanded to
regular participation in Sunday's Bread, a weekly opportu-

nity for members to prepare and serve a hot meal to [the] city's homeless and hungry. The progression, which the rabbis characterized in traditional terms as *mitzvah goreret mitzvah* (one mitzvah inspires the next), was symbolically important as a move towards increased personal involvement in community service.

The same progression was evident in action for Soviet Jewry during the 1980s. At first the two rabbis went alone to visit refusniks in the Soviet Union. Then, they decided to involve the congregation. The first step was to ask congregants to send with them needed goods, including medical supplies, for Soviet Jews. The second step was to organize trips in which congregants went to meet refusniks and other Soviet Jews. The third step was to organize a campaign to help win the release of specific families and individuals from the Soviet Union. The final step was to help settle the Jews who arrived in the area and integrate those who were interested into the life of the synagogue.

Norman and Don were accurate in assessing that the center was alive on this issue and that congregants would be drawn into helping Soviet Jews, but the numbers who became directly involved were relatively limited. The circle, though, did not close with that intense involvement. During the year of this study, when the struggle to free Jews from the still-existent Soviet Union was ongoing, Norman would announce towards the end of the services I attended that there were postcards available at the back of the room that were addressed to Soviet officials on behalf of individual Jews who had not been allowed to emigrate. Each postcard had on it the photo of the individuals involved. Norman invited each participant in the service to fill out a postcard before leaving.

He did this with urgency in his voice and impressed on his congregation the human need that would be served and the mitzvah that would be fulfilled. I thought: He does not want anyone to leave the service without having the opportunity to be directly involved. His message was clearly educational. Having now participated in Jewish worship, congregants should realize that Judaism is a participatory religion in which the individual is asked to move beyond words to concrete action. Norman believes each selected mitzvah presents an opportunity to do some good and to reach for a higher spiritual plane.

Educating the Congregation

In holding up those postcards, Norman was humanizing the institution and educating the congregants. The faces of the refusniks conveyed how personal an act was involved. But the language of mitzvah is educational in nature. He was attempting, as he did when teaching midrash, to frame ethical and spiritual imperatives in explicitly traditional terms. He recalled in conversation that the first sermon he ever gave on Soviet Jewry in 1966 was framed entirely as a call for civil rights. Today he speaks of mitzvot to teach congregants to act Jewishly through the language of tradition.

In the rabbis' program for revitalizing Temple Akiba, education is the natural extension of community-building. No longer satisfied to build the synagogue community around social action alone, the rabbis look to education to provide their congregants with a Jewish language to frame the moral and spiritual activities they share in common. *Jewish values* are not simply today's politically correct actions. They are "a resource bank of values and behaviors" which informs one's actions as a Jew.[14]

In the rabbis' view, special emphasis needs to be placed on adult education in the synagogue, for if community-building entails learning a new Jewish language, adults have to be educated in that language. Belonging to and participating in the synagogue community will have little meaning if the members are not learning and growing as Jews. To provide those growth opportunities, Temple Akiba has developed a broad menu of adult educational offerings which include: three weekly Torah study sessions offered by the rabbis, adult Bar or Bat Mitzvah study, a monthly luncheon for seniors, several lecture series, a dinner and discussion group for post-college young adults, family education for parents and children, and an educational outreach group for intermarried couples and Jews-by-choice.

Temple Akiba has offered a wide range of activities for adults since the 1920s. What Rabbis Davidman and Marcus have added is an explicit focus on the relation between social activity and Jewish learning—the realization that in synagogue life community-building and Jewish education are highly correlated activities. This relationship works in two directions. Social occasions that the temple would want to sponsor, such as bringing the parents of young children together, are given a religious-educational dimension by turning the event into "Shabbat is for Kids," a monthly Shabbat service for the parents and children. Educational formats, such as Torah study, become opportunities for community-building because everyone in the room is addressed on a first-name basis and the regularity of meeting allows people to socialize as well as study.

An educational consultant explained the temple's rationale for stressing adult education. She said Temple Akiba was unique in this metropolitan area regarding the rabbi's insistence that Jewish education is for people of all ages and not essentially for children. Although the Temple Akiba school and youth program are as good as any, the rabbis do not stress those programs alone. They want the members to feel that what is offered to the children educationally is not essentially different from what is offered to the adults. The rabbis are building a Jewish community for a diverse population—diverse in age as well as in socio-economic status and religious background. To build that community they have to educate all the members, young and old, because very few of the adults have received the Jewish education they need to participate as fully informed members of the community. If the children enter with minimal Jewish knowledge, the adults enter with only slightly more, some of which has faded with time and distance.

Worship

Worship at Temple Akiba has been undergoing successive revisions since the nineteenth century.[15] In more recent years the shift has been toward an increase in congregational participation and the use of Hebrew in the service. To be an active participant one needs to know some Hebrew. A parent on the school committee told me she felt she had to learn Hebrew now—an option not available to her during childhood—because without that knowledge, she was an outsider to her own prayer services.

Cantor Richard Perry is the embodiment of the new style in worship service. A man in his thirties, Richard is best known for the guitar he uses in services. Jewish music at Temple Akiba, which has been experiencing a revival, draws heavily from the folk music tradition of the 1960s and 1970s. At services, Richard, inevitably dressed in the businessman suit that is the standard clergy uniform, stands up on the *bimah* of the main sanctuary and leads the congregation in a folk melody for a Hebrew prayer.

More than one form of music is used at services. Richard leads three different choirs: a professional one, an adult member choir, and a children's choir. He also joins with the rabbis in creating a number of different liturgies for different kinds of services. In fact, variety has become a hallmark of worship at Temple Akiba. On some Friday nights there are late services, which are usually held in the main sanctuary. On other Friday nights, Kabbalat Shabbat, the traditional Friday evening service, begins at 5:45 P.M. and is held in more intimate quarters to give the feeling of praying with a smaller community.

In a two-month period in the winter, there were five different Friday night services. Each had a different theme and slightly varied liturgy. The themes related to Jewish book month, life after forty, family worship, hunger and homelessness, and *Shabbat Shirah*, the Sabbath of song. The variation is designed to attract different constituencies and to stress that worship is not an isolated phenomenon within synagogue life. The various services allow the clergy to educate the congregation about the resources within the tradition. Kabbalat Shabbat provides an education within a traditional prayer format. A service on hunger and homelessness teaches the traditional basis for contemporary commitments to social action.

The design of the whole worship experience communicates the rabbis' essential vision that community, education, and worship are three integrally related aspects of religious life of Temple Akiba. Rabbis Davidman and Marcus view themselves as having led a transformation in all three aspects of synagogue life that together have revitalized Jewish life at Temple Akiba.

Seliḥot: **Educating through Worship**

During the summer between my two years of field work, I received a call from Don Marcus in which he asked me if I would be willing to work with Rachel Abeles, the newly appointed assistant rabbi, in planning and implementing the study session that precedes the *Seliḥot* service. *Seliḥot* are the penitential prayers that are traditionally recited the Saturday night before Rosh Hashanah to help prepare the congregation to enter the solemn mood of the High Holidays.

Don thought I could be helpful to Rachel in planning the type of program she was envisioning. As I was anxious to meet the new rabbi and gain an inside view of the rabbis' planning process, I agreed to modify my research role and work with Rabbi Abeles.[16]

I met with Rachel in her office on a hot July day. She wanted to get a head start on this program. It would be the first program of the holiday season that she would be leading. This was her first congregational position, and as the first woman rabbi in this temple's history, she may have been feeling some extra pressure to do well.[17] Yet I found her calm and open to discussing the details of the panel that she wished to put together.

We decided that Rachel would assemble a panel of three congregants who would prepare a short personal statement on their thoughts about entering the High Holiday season. The focus was to be on the internal preparation that these holidays call for. I was to phone the three congregants, give them encouragement, and prepare a statement of my own that would summarize and comment on their personal statements. Rachel would serve as the moderator for the program.

When I arrived that Saturday evening in September Rabbi Abeles appeared nervous. She introduced me to the three panelists with whom I had spoken on the phone. I learned that our program would be held in the chapel, to be followed by a coffee hour in the social hall and then the service in the atrium.

As we entered, the chapel was already full, with about two hundred people. Rabbi Abeles, the panelists, and I walked up to the front and took our prearranged seats. I could see Rabbis Davidman and Marcus sitting off to the side among the congregants.

Rachel introduced the program and each of us. Jacqueline, the first to speak, is a tall, striking woman with white hair. Her tone was immediately personal. We learned of her love for her father, who used to say he would fast for her on Yom Kippur since she finds it so difficult. She shared her hope that as she grows older she could develop the courage to follow her own heart and pursue her own interests. I heard an older woman letting us in on some of the struggles she now faces.

Paul is a thin, bespectacled man in his forties, a successful doctor. He shared personal memories of sitting with his father at High Holiday services and, in turn, his thoughts about sitting with his own children at more recent services. He spoke of his conflict about taking these days off from work when many other Jewish doctors do not. Yet for him these gatherings of family and community cut to the core of what it means to be Jewish.

Ellen, a pleasant-looking woman in her late twenties, a lawyer by profession, was the most knowledgeable Jewishly of the three. She spoke of the significance of sitting with family at services and of having grown up in the synagogue that she still attends. She also spoke of the prayers themselves and of the music. She has sung in a Hebrew choir and relates deeply to the music of the holidays and the messages the musical prayers convey.

I tied together some of the themes they raised by talking about the rhythms of the seasons and the relation between the passing of summer, the coming of fall, and the turn inward to self-reflection and penitence. After I concluded, Rabbi Abeles took back the microphone and invited reflections and questions from the floor.

What surprised me about what followed was the search for Jewish knowledge expressed in the questions and comments. The panel had been personal in focus, but the congregants wanted more information about the evening's ritual. Why is the service called *Selihot?* Why is it held at midnight? What is its relation to *havdalah?* One man, Jacqueline's husband, spoke of his growing appreciation for traditional practices that he did not always practice. He compared fasting on Yom Kippur to keeping kosher and spoke of them as necessary spiritual disciplines.

The hour flew by and Rachel closed the program. Norman then rose to speak for the first time. He thanked Rabbi Abeles for having organized this event and expressed his appreciation for the work she had done. Then he spoke of a refusnik family in need of help and of the postcards to be sent out.

Everyone went across to the social hall for a coffee-and-cake reception. The coffee and tea were set up in large silver urns that sit on tables covered with white table-cloths. People were served by the women from the sisterhood who were behind the tables. There was a feeling of being at an elegant reception.

At 11:00 P.M. everyone filed out of the social hall and climbed the stairs to the atrium that stands between the main sanctuary and the auditorium. The atrium has a very tall glass ceiling that at night becomes a reflecting surface. As people found their places in the rows of folding chairs, Rabbi Davidman explained that since this was Saturday night, they would begin with *havdalah.* On every chair was a *havdalah* candle. Rabbis Marcus and Abeles each had a very large lit candle and went around the room lighting all the other candles. With over two hundred candles lit, and all of the light being reflected off the glass ceiling, one felt engulfed by the *havdalah* flame as the prayer was recited.

On each chair was also a printed booklet of the *Selihot* service prepared by the clergy of Temple Akiba. It contained a mixture of the traditional *Seliḥot* prayers in Hebrew with contemporary English readings reflecting the penitential mood. Cantor Perry sang the Hebrew prayers. Each English reading was read by a family who came up to the front and led the prayer. I later learned these were the families of the tenth-graders who made up the Confirmation class. The service took about an hour, and shortly after midnight everyone quietly left the synagogue.

It had been a full evening, and I had my own reactions to sort out. But quite apart from how it felt to be a participant in a Temple Akiba program, the evening illustrated many of the elements of the rabbis' vision for this synagogue. The evening's program showed how community, worship, and education can complement each other in an educating synagogue.

The idea to create a panel of congregants was Rachel's, but the plan to have a study session precede the worship was a Davidman-Marcus design. Rachel added to their design the psychological dimension of entering the mood of the season. She wanted to sponsor dialogue among congregants to build community around common, shared Jewish experiences. While the panelists each confessed that he or she had never before spoken publicly of these experiences, they were well chosen. They represented different age groups within the congregation but spoke as individuals. When Jacqueline and Paul spoke of the struggles they still experience about whether to take off these days or fast on Yom Kippur, their personal comments had a strong effect.

The questions posed by the congregants reflected the ongoing nature of the adult educational process. These type of *Seliḥot* prayers are a relatively new addition to the synagogue's liturgy. Their late-evening timing is anomalous. As with the Passover seder, much about *Seliḥot* raises questions for the curious. That the adults were free to ask questions without having to feign knowledge testifies to an atmosphere that encourages Jewish learning.

The reception in the social hall was an important part of the evening. It allowed the sisterhood its traditional role of providing a certain elegance critical to the historical identity of Temple Akiba. The event also allowed people to socialize. *Seliḥot* is often the first event in which people see each other after the summer, and it serves as a social occasion for people to catch up with one another.

At Temple Akiba *havdalah* is not a weekly event. There are no weekly services to close out the Shabbat as there are at more traditional synagogues. But the rabbis clearly planned the *havdalah* ritual to take place in the dark atrium where the reflecting ceiling created a very powerful effect. As good choreographers of a ritual performance, they were using the props and the backdrop to magnify the visual impact of *havdalah*. In fact, the use of the candles continued throughout the recitation of the *Seliḥot* service. The clergy were borrowing from *havdalah* to give *Seliḥot* an extra degree of drama.

But there were also educational messages in the *Seliḥot* liturgy itself. The creation of the service booklet reflected the temple's self-perception as a designer of its own liturgical style. The alternation between the Hebrew prayers and the English readings reflected the balance they try to establish between the traditional and the modern. So, too, did the cantor's alternating between formal cantorial chanting and informal Hebrew folksinging reflect a balance of formality and informality. Finally, the inclusion of the high school students and their parents demonstrated clearly the tie between the worship ritual of the synagogue and the educational program of the school. Here were youth who will be completing their eleventh year of religious education coming up to read the first prayers of the new year. Here were parents and children participating together as families in a ritual that has as one of its main themes continuity across generations.

Barbara Myerhoff has noted that "rituals and ceremonies are cultural mirrors, opportunities for representing collective knowledge"(p.32). The *Seliḥot* evening provided the Temple Akiba clergy with a grand opportunity to mirror for their congregants images of their temple as an educating community. The rituals invite a number of the constituent groups within the synagogue to display their identity as participants in this community. The panelists, the adult learners in the chapel, the new assistant, and the two senior rabbis, the sisterhood, the cantor, the school children, and their parents all had their way of displaying their identities within this congregation. Equally important, the synagogue culture itself was on display. In this carefully planned, three-part ceremony, one could see much of "the sacred story" of Temple Akiba being performed by the participants in the ritual. As Myerhoff observes, "Enacted beliefs have a capacity for arousing belief that mere statements do not. . . . Ritual and ceremony generate conviction when reason and thought may fail" (p.32).

Finally, this was Rabbi Abeles' night, her debut, but this was very understated in terms of public display. Aside from Norman's warm appreciation of the work she invested, there was little else to draw attention to her. Yet there was a quiet pride in the change, in the selection of a first woman rabbi. And Rachel played the role to perfection for this synagogue. That she had clearly done her homework well was reflected in the smooth flow of the session with the panel. She could take charge and yet let others speak. She could also blend in well with the clergy team as she did during the *havdalah* and *Selihot* services. A presence, but part of the whole; change within continuity of style. These are elements of the cultural identity that Temple Akiba wishes to reflect.

Family Education

If ritual and ceremony serve as cultural mirrors, the *Selihot* study and worship service presented an ideal image of Temple Akiba. Everything worked together beautifully that night; rabbinic vision and synagogue reality were closely in sync. But, Myerhoff warns, these "reflections are not always accurate." Cultural mirrors may "alter images, sometimes distorting, sometimes disguising various features"(p.33). *Selihot*, taken alone, would be distorting, for there is more complexity and tension in the relation between vision and reality in Temple Akiba than was revealed through this service. Some of that complexity and tension will become more evident in considering the family education session (described later in this chapter) in which Rabbi Marcus played a significant role.

Family education is a recent movement in synagogue education to include parents along with children in teaching and celebrating Judaism. It begins with the recognition that parents and other family members often feel themselves without much of a connection to Judaism and are open to learning more as their children are receiving their own religious education. Family education programs welcome parents to join their children in the synagogue— often on Sunday mornings—to learn about Jewish subjects that are of mutual interest to adults and children.[18]

Although Temple Akiba was not a pioneer in this field, this year the Temple Akiba educators were planning family education programs more systematically than before for many of the grades in the school. Rabbi Marcus had asked Molly Siegel, a senior educator in the religious school, to take charge of planning these educational programs. The sixth-grade program was the third on the calendar for this year. It centered on Judaism's view of death and dying, a topic that fit well into the Jewish life cycle course that the sixth-graders were taking on Sunday mornings.

The program was scheduled to run during the first two periods of the religious school day. This schedule left third period as a time when Molly and Don could sit with the parents to evaluate the program. The program had been planned by Molly and the sixth-grade teachers to involve parents and children in an active exploration of different aspects of the topic. Each teacher would set up a center of study in a different corner of the social hall. Molly would run a center on the feelings experienced around death; Janice would run one on the Jewish rituals for the period of death and mourning; Saul would run a third on public expressions of sorrow such as eulogies, obituaries, and letters of condolence. The whole group of students and parents would be divided into three equal-size groups, and each group would make the rounds learning at the three centers.

When I arrived that morning at 10:00 A.M., the eighteen parents and close to fifty children had already assembled in the social hall. Rabbi Marcus was about to introduce the program. Soon they were divided into three groups, and I attached myself to one. There were seventy minutes for this rotation, with twenty or so minutes for each center. My group started at Molly's center and then went to Janice's and Saul's.

The stop at Janice's center would prove decisive for the fate of this program. Janice explained that she would be focusing on the Jewish customs "that help get us through the process of mourning." She began discussing *shivah,* the traditional seven days after the funeral during which the family of the deceased sits together to receive comfort from visitors who come daily to share their grief and speak of the deceased.[19] In contemporary American Jewish life there are many variations on this tradition, including shortening the period to three days or observing it in less prescribed ways.

Janice asked how many in the group had visited a *shivah.* Only the parents raised their hands. Janice then asked if they had seen customs at a *shivah* that they had not understood, but first assured them: "It's not that everyone does them [the customs] or has to do them. Every family chooses."

The group was quite ready to ask about customs they had seen or heard about. Parents and children chimed in, asking about customs from both funerals and *shivah,* including the mourners wearing black ribbons and tearing their clothes, opening or not opening the casket, saying the *Kaddish* (the mourner's prayer), and bringing the food when visiting a *shivah.* Each time, a member of the group would raise a custom for consideration and Janice or others would briefly explain it. Then Janice returned to what they specifically had seen at a *shivah.* The parents mentioned customs such as covering the mirrors, sitting on crates or low benches, and the mourners not wearing shoes. One mother very poignantly shared with the group that when her husband had died, she did not know what to do. The rabbis, she said, were very helpful in suggesting how to structure the mourning period.

At some point during this give-and-take, Don, who

had gone upstairs to attend to the rest of the school, returned to the social hall and was standing at the back of this group. Noticing him, Janice said, "Rabbi Marcus has joined us. He will explain not wearing shoes [at the *shivah*]." I was taken by surprise, and I believe Don was too. There did not seem to be any call from the group to have this custom explained.

As Don moved to the front a quiet descended on the group. All eyes were on him. I realized that this man whom I call Don Marcus was "Rabbi" to them. He was stepping into the rabbi role with a lot of authority attached. Perhaps realizing that, Don did not directly answer the question, but took them on a brief journey through Jewish traditional thinking about death and contact with the dead. The quick give-and-take between group and leader had given way to a conceptually oriented discourse on death in Judaism.

When he finished this brief discourse, Don was immediately faced with a slew of questions about the rationale for traditional mourning customs. The parents and children seemed to have a stored-up curiosity about these customs that they could now raise with the rabbi. Realizing he would go well beyond her request, Don checked with Janice, who agreed to his continuing for the few minutes left in this rotation. There was clearly a great deal of interest in this subject.

In answering these questions, Don continued for the most part to explain traditional rather than modern Reform practice. Among the concepts he explained was "first degree relations," or the traditional definition of who is obligated in laws of mourning. He explained that Jewish tradition names seven relatives: mother, father, son, daughter, sister, brother, and husband or wife. When any of these members of the family dies, one has a traditional obligation to mourn, which includes sitting *shivah*.

Time was quickly up and the group moved on to Saul's center. After the three rotations were over, the children left with Janice and Saul, and the parents joined Molly and the rabbi for a feedback session. This was the first year this kind of program had been tried, and Molly wanted to get parental reaction.

The parents' reactions were positive but mixed. Several, saying such discussions are hard to do at home and that schools usually do not tackle the issue of death, expressed real appreciation for the opportunity to discuss these matters with their children. They liked the format of the three centers, the movement around the hall, and the way the teachers handled the questions raised. But there were also procedural complaints. The mailing to the parents had not been clear. They were not sure what to expect. Perhaps some parents did not show up because they did not realize what the program would be.

All this feedback was delivered in calm voices. Then Marcia spoke up. She began calmly enough by saying the program had been empowering to her child and herself, but then she turned to Rabbi Marcus and became more agitated. Referring to his explanation about "the first degree relations," she said, "Many of the kids do not come from the traditional family configuration." That began quite a heated exchange that other parents joined as she started to accuse the rabbi of insensitivity to the needs of children from nontraditional families.

> *Marcia: But they [these children] feel invalidated. They feel it [mourning] won't count for the stepparent or the parent's lover.*
>
> *Rabbi: It's really important to do both things, to say what is traditional Judaism and what we represent.*
>
> *Sally: You are saying these people are "others."*
>
> *Becky: It is all relative to who is important to you. They [the children] can apply the principles without putting confines on them.*
>
> *Marcia: We can do that, but not the kids.*
>
> *Rabbi: In so many ways we open up and expand the tradition. Everything about this place and school is intended to do that.*
>
> *Marcia: I recognize and value that.*
>
> *Rabbi: But you cannot rewrite an answer that is two thousand years old. That is fact. Then you move beyond that and apply it to the life of the individual. It's a failure to do one and not the other. We don't want to deny the historical fact.*

Becky: Are you teaching the value of the nuclear family?
*Bill: You were asked a neutral question and answered
from the perspective of tradition.*
*Rabbi: When I do my work as a rabbi with a family, I
immediately expand the definition of mourner and family.
For example, [I include as mourners] friends who feel primary. In liberal Judaism I feel it is important to extend that
[designation of mourner] to any imaginable family situation. We instinctively expand that. But you do have to say
what tradition says. I can't put "significant other" in the
mouth of tradition. We have to know what it says in its
own right. But with all the kids we have to be sensitive to
the fact that someone else's reality is not the same as yours.
I affirm that fully.*

With that last statement, the heated exchange ended,
and Molly turned the conversation back to appraising the
program. But it did not end there for Don. When we
walked out together after the program, he told me he was
very upset and had no idea why he had been attacked. He
wanted to get back to Marcia, a woman with whom he had
a relationship, to find out why she so suddenly went on
the attack.

I believe Don was upset not just about the suddenness
of Marcia's attack, but also that it came from her. As he
would later tell me, Marcia is a single mother who has a
significant other. Her former husband is no longer
involved in child care. She had come previously to speak
to Don, and he had encouraged her to join the temple and
send her child to the school. She knew of his personal commitment and the synagogue's policy regarding welcoming
nontraditional families. Why, then, would she publicly
accuse him of being insensitive and of invalidating these
children?

When we spoke later in the week, Don told me he had
called Marcia that afternoon and shared with her his surprise and hurt. She acknowledged there were other personal issues motivating her behavior. Don invited her to
have a conversation with him on these issues and she
agreed. That left him feeling more resolved about their

relationship. He closed our conversation by saying, "You never know what will walk in the door here." When you are a rabbi and an educator, you can never tell what personal baggage people will bring to their relationship with you. But Don works hard to develop close personal ties with parents. He opens himself up to them and makes himself vulnerable to their expressed feelings. He sees this as an important piece of educational work. Marcia's attack hurt him but did not dissuade him from continuing his relationship with her.

Social Drama

I felt challenged by what I had observed that morning. Sitting with the group in Janice's center, I could feel viscerally, as I reported in Chapter 1, the group's intense involvement with the material and excitement at sharing a close moment with Rabbi Marcus. I was therefore not prepared for the emotional turn of the tide the next hour when the rabbi's comments became the subject of heated controversy. I also was surprised by the flow of events: how quickly the tone changed, how other parents joined in Marcia's objections, and then how suddenly the controversy ended and Molly could return to the business at hand.

On reflection, I realized that although Don focused on Marcia, I had to see this turn of events in larger terms. Something of significance had occurred within this group of parents and within the family education program. In thinking through the sequence of events, I recognized that they fit Victor Turner's description of a "social drama" well—a dramatic conflict between members of an organization that begins with a breach in the normative order, draws in the other participants, and progresses in a sequence from the spread to the resolution of the crisis. Following Turner's schema, we can recast the events in the following sequence:

1. When Rabbi Marcus was invited to address the group on the Jewish customs of mourning, he

unknowingly breached the norms of the group by explaining these customs from a traditional perspective, one that seemed to be endorsing the traditional family configuration as normative.

2. The interchange in the group became a crisis when Marcia turned on the rabbi with a sudden degree of heat. Her saying that he had invalidated the children who come from nontraditional families was the critical point. In a temple where outreach and inclusion are the declared norms, the rabbi who is perceived to breach that norm is in an untenable position.

3. The crisis spread in two ways. By standing his ground and insisting that Jewish tradition must be allowed to speak in its own voice, the rabbi seemed to be unapologetically accepting its endorsement of the traditional nuclear family. That prompted other parents to join Marcia and accuse the rabbi of treating these people as "others" and teaching "the value of the nuclear family." In a liberal community, that is very questionable behavior.

4. The immediate crisis was resolved only when the rabbi switched from defending traditional language to describing also how in their current practice the rabbis of this synagogue use a very expansive definition of family in deciding who is a mourner. Only when the parents heard him endorsing their shared liberal views as his own could they allow the exchange to end and return to considering what they shared of the morning's program. For Don the crisis was resolved only later when he and Marcia had reestablished their personal relationship.

By recasting this heated exchange as a social drama, we can better understand the sequence of events and, more importantly, what was at stake in the exchange. This analysis moves attention away from the psychological question, Why did Marcia act this way? to the cultural question, What does this teach us about this synagogue's culture?

Had Marcia been speaking only for herself, this

would have been a two-person exchange that the rest of the group would have silently watched. But what made this exchange a crisis was that Marcia's objection highlighted a value conflict that many in the group felt. By speaking primarily about mourners from a traditional Jewish view, Don was engaging in an educational exercise that paralleled Norman's teaching in the Torah study group. He was teaching congregants categories of traditional Jewish thought with which they had little familiarity. He was deepening their Jewish knowledge base.

However, in taking this educational step with a group of parents who were unfamiliar with and unprepared for the new curriculum of the rabbis, Don breached the norm of inclusiveness that is widely held in the congregation. I doubt he did so intentionally; but once Marcia picked up on his traditional language, and Don stood his ground in defense of that language, the crisis was ignited. Then the other parents were quickly drawn in and felt the need to defend the norm of inclusiveness that he had breached.

One could ask why Don did not realize he was breaching this norm or why he stood with the language of the tradition when others were so clear in their objections. But standing firm is the whole point. As a rabbi and educator in this synagogue, he firmly believes, along with Norman and Rachel, in the educational importance of representing a traditional perspective to a contemporary audience. He expects that knowledge of tradition will not sit comfortably at times with his congregants. Yet he risks their discomfort in presenting this knowledge.

At the same time, Don is a liberal rabbi who in practice is not bound by traditional halakhah. He believes in inclusiveness—in welcoming the nontraditional family and in "extending that [designation of mourner] to any imaginable family situation." In practice he stands with his congregants and their contemporary values. When he articulates the principles of his practice, Don is able to resolve this crisis. He comes over to their side and hears their issues from their contemporary perspective.

Yet, had Rabbi Marcus immediately jumped to his actual practice and distanced himself from the voice of the tradition, I believe he would have shortcut the learning process for these parents. Put simply: *the social drama was itself a learning experience.* Had Marcia not raised her fierce objection and Rabbi Marcus not stood his ground, there still would have been meaningful learning about Judaism, death, and mourning. But the tension of the social drama added a whole other dimension to the learning. As one mother in the group, whom I knew as a prominent educator in the secular world, reported to me: "I learned the temple has standards; it stands for something." Though she too was taken by surprise by the turn of events, she felt reassured by the rabbi's standing his ground. His enacted message took on particular meaning.

On the other hand, Marcia also had a point. As a single mother who is raising her child with her unmarried significant other, she knows that her lifestyle is not endorsed by traditional Judaism. She may feel that Jewish tradition—in its code for mourning as well as elsewhere—is not friendly to many of her most deeply held contemporary convictions. Thus, when the rabbi, who welcomed her into this community and implicitly conveyed the message that her values would be respected here, taught that there are only seven relatives for whom you are obligated to mourn, she may have felt confused and even betrayed. What about the significant other who is also a parent? Is he or she not to be mourned?

Turner and Myerhoff have shown that identifying a crisis as a social drama can be very instructive in illuminating some of the normative contradictions within a culture.[20] We have seen how the Temple Akiba rabbis have moved in two directions simultaneously. They have built community by reaching out to diverse constituencies and incorporating them within the synagogue community. They have also worked to educate that community to become increasingly knowledgeable about Jewish tradition so that in situations such as death in the family, members will understand how Jewish tradition can be a valuable resource for them.

For the most part, congregants have been satisfied to follow the rabbis' lead in moving in both these directions. Yet here is a case, and not an isolated one, in which the two directions come into conflict. Through the lens of the social drama the conflict of values—the contradictory tendencies—come powerfully to light. How can the same rabbis who so proudly teach the values of rabbinic Judaism also be so welcoming to nontraditional families whom that tradition would not normatively affirm?

Don did not answer that question directly, but the way he played his role in the social drama can be viewed as his enacted answer. Through his actions he conveyed a message of his working on the integration of these conflicting tendencies. He refused to put terms like "significant other" "in the mouth of tradition" because, he said, "We have to know what it says in its own right." Yet, in explaining his actual rabbinic practice and in his continued reaching out to Marcia, he let everyone know that he, a defender of the faith, puts people ahead of traditionalism.

Myerhoff has also taught that the presence of value conflict and social drama is not a sign of cultural weakness, for almost all cultures "are ridden with internal inconsistencies" (p. 33). Participants in a culture learn to live with the inconsistencies and barely notice them—that is, until a crisis like this brings them to the fore. Then they need to be addressed and somehow reconciled.

But reconciliation is not a logical move. Cultures do not function as logical systems, but more like what Myerhoff calls "a *tsimmes*"—"a curious mixture" in which "the old ingredients are mixed with the new" (p. 151). A social drama does not conclude with a new teaching, but with an affirmation that, for all the conflicts and contradictions, the members of this cultural unit will continue to cohere as a community in which people value one another. Through this social drama Rabbi Marcus showed himself to be both committed to tradition and caring of people. If his commitment and caring are not logically in balance, their dramatic integration remains convincing enough to restore the harmony and redress the imbalance that set off this crisis.

Chapter 3

The Temple Akiba School

At 9:30 A.M. of the first Sunday of the school year, Rabbi Don Marcus looks out at the faces of his faculty gathered for teacher orientation. He will begin the orientation by speaking on Reform Judaism and will leave much of the nuts and bolts of school life to the three coordinators, or head teachers, who help manage the Temple Akiba school. But first everyone is to introduce himself. Don begins.

I have been here since 1978—five years on the pulpit side with the youth program. In 1983 I moved over to the school side. It was the last "never." [In rabbinical school] I swore I'd never work in a synagogue, never in a big synagogue, and never in religious education. But circumstances play funny tricks on you.

After Don, the three coordinators introduce themselves:

Ann: This is my second year. I love it here. I am the Hebrew coordinator, which includes the Melton program, tutorials and non-Hebrew students.[1]

Molly: This is my seventh year here. I coordinate grades four through eight and do sociodrama in the high school on Monday nights. I commute all the way from [a city over the state line]; that's how much I love this place.

Ruth: At twenty-plus years it's got to be love. I coordinate the primary grades and train teachers at [a local college].

In the structure of the Temple Akiba school, the coordinators serve as the middle level of management. They work most closely with the teachers on classroom teaching and curriculum. Having taught first grade in the Sunday school for many years before assuming the coordinator position shortly after Don became the educator, Ruth is the veteran. Her specialty is early childhood education. Molly, a drama therapist, was teaching in the school when Don became educator and moved into this position several years ago. Ann taught Hebrew in other local synagogue schools and came to Temple Akiba last year to fill the Hebrew coordinator position.

After the coordinators, Betty, the synagogue librarian, introduces herself. She is followed by the twelve teachers present. There are twenty-one classroom teachers on the Sunday school faculty, but primarily the new teachers have come for this first hour. Of these, nine are women and three are men; most are young teachers in their twenties. Only two teachers—one of whom grew up at Temple Akiba—identify themselves as products of the Reform movement.

Given the difficulty of finding qualified teachers for the school, Rabbi Marcus chooses to cast a wide net and to find teachers who do not necessarily identify as Reform Jews. Yet he wants to offer the teachers some sense of contemporary Reform Judaism. He is not preaching the gospel of Reform, but orienting teachers of diverse backgrounds to the changing religious practices of Temple Akiba.

Without a note in hand, Don sets out to explain four theological issues: the significance of mitzvot, the approach to sacred text, the place of theological language in religious education, and the meaning of the messiah. These are complex issues, but he is a fluent presenter. Sitting with the teachers, I am taken by the intellectual force of his words, but I am not sure the teachers are. Only one teacher raises a question—on the Reform view of the Bible. Otherwise, the teachers listen quietly to this intellectually abstract presentation. But that distance recedes as Don turns to discussing the Reform approach to intermarriage and inclusiveness.

> You will discover in your classroom and in the Reform movement that the welcome mat is laid open

to the children of families in which one parent is not Jewish. In Reform halakhah,[2] if we consider the child of a Jewish mother to be Jewish, so too is the child of a Jewish father.

A controversial decision was taken by the Reform movement in 1983 to consider the child of a Jewish father in an intermarriage to be Jewish just as the child of a Jewish mother is.[3] The decision is controversial for it departs from the traditional understanding that Jewishness is conveyed to a child only through the status of the mother. But in following its principles of treating men and women equally and welcoming intermarried couples, the Reform movement decided to define all the children of an intermarried couple as potentially Jewish without requiring conversion as would be the case in a Conservative or Orthodox synagogue.

Don continues: "A condition of your teaching here is to view all of the children here as Jews because that is how they view themselves." For the first time a condition of employment is laid down. Given the division within contemporary Jewry over how to define who is a Jew, with only the Reform and Reconstructionist movements embracing all the children of intermarriages as potentially Jewish without conversion, Don knows some teachers may not consider the children of non-Jewish mothers to be Jewish. Yet he is insisting that whatever their private views, as teachers at Temple Akiba they need to affirm the Jewishness of all the children. That, far more than their view of the Bible or of the messianic age, is critical to their working in this synagogue school.

Inclusiveness, Don continues, goes beyond acceptance of the children of the intermarried:

> Within Reform, and especially here, we extend welcome to gays and lesbians. There are children in the school whose parents are gay or lesbian. Dealing with our own attitudes on this issue is important, including the language and texts we use. Significant numbers of the kids are not living the lives of tradi-

tional families, including kids from single-parent homes and blended families. It is not what we endorse, but what we support. We support kids and use a variety of models to match the diversity of the population. The diversity here is as great as in any synagogue in America. That includes interracial kids and kids from homes of wealth and homes of near poverty.

Given its look of wealth, Temple Akiba can be deceiving to new teachers who may not realize that the temple's philosophy of inclusiveness has attracted a broader diversity of children than one might expect to see in a synagogue. In my first year of observing, I often was surprised by the diversity of family names and the number of children who "don't look Jewish."[4] If, like many American Jews, these teachers have been conditioned to believe they know what Jews look like, some of the children in Temple Akiba will take them by surprise. Don is helping to prepare them for meeting the children.

Beyond the diversity of names and appearances lies the less visible, but no less powerful, changes in family lifestyles. It is common to assume that most children in the school come from American Jewish families with two married parents in the home. That is often not the case, however, and it is a challenge to find the language that includes the nontraditional household within the Jewish definition of *family*.[5]

As soon as Don finishes, Bonnie, a teacher new to this school, picks up on the issue of children of intermarried parents and their celebrating Jewish and Christian holidays. Her comments ignite a rush of interchange among Don, Molly, and the teachers. Listening to the deep uncertainty that these teachers express over how to respond to students who come from families that celebrate both Christmas and Hanukkah, I wonder, why is this concern surfacing so powerfully this early in the year? Why does children's talk about Christmas put the teachers on edge? Did Don intend to bring this point of tension to the surface so early in the year? What does this interchange teach us about the school at Temple Akiba?

This chapter and the next focus on questions such as these. The aim is to understand the culture of this synagogue school: both what makes this school work as it does and what makes it challenging for teachers to teach and students to learn. For if the literature on synagogue schools leaves but one impression, it is that the tasks of teaching and learning are made difficult by the cultural context—by the ambivalent position of educators presenting Judaism to American Jews.

At this orientation, Don brings the cultural context into the conversation, and everyone reacts with marked ambivalence. Although not every synagogue school faces the diversity in student body that Temple Akiba has chosen for itself, they all face the task of having to bridge the children's cultural reality and the world of Jewish tradition as the synagogue understands it. There is a palpable cultural tension built into the Jewish classroom; the teacher will be presenting to the children aspects of Judaism with which they are not familiar and making normative claims about the significance of these aspects—the Hebrew language, the prayers, the ritual objects for celebration—that are largely unsupported by the children's experience outside the school. David Schoem has written that attending a synagogue school represents "a kind of 'stepping out' of one's routine of life to provide some small link with one's heritage" (pp. 28–29).

Jewish schools have adopted different strategies for dealing with these cultural tensions. Writing about Orthodox yeshivot for *Baalei Teshuvah,* Janet Aviad has described "their offensive against secular culture." The rabbis of the yeshivot are as clear in their opposition to all that secular culture represents as fundamentalist Christians are to secular humanism. This clear ideological opposition calls for an educational strategy of detachment from the snares of secularism, absorption into a total environment of Orthodox Jewish practice, and a re-creation of the self in the image of one's newfound ideals and relationships.[6]

Having neither the ideological zeal nor the total environment of these yeshivot, the synagogue school is based on a more accommodating relationship to secular culture. Yet within these parameters, various approaches to the cultural tensions are possible. Although laying claim to only a small portion of the children's time and energy, the educators may choose either to maximize or minimize the observable differences between the world of the synagogue and the world "out there."

Differences may be maximized by behavioral, cognitive, and affective strategies. A child entering a synagogue school may be asked to put on a kippah if he is a boy, to be called by a Hebrew name, and to engage in activities— such as formal prayer—that rarely go on outside the synagogue. The child may learn a new language—Hebrew— and a set of religious terms derived from the tradition that are not often heard in the outside world. The child may also be placed in situations in which strong emotions are aroused about being Jewish, about feeling attached to the Jewish people and feeling separate or different from people who are not Jewish.[7]

A maximizing approach stresses the differences that separate Jews from non-Jews and Judaism from other religions. Many of the activities sponsored and much of the content taught will be in the service of providing the children—and when possible, their families—with the cultural knowledge to lead as full Jewish lives as possible within the context of a multicultural, secular society. This approach is not at war with secular culture, but it seeks to carve out islands of Jewish living within that culture.

December is a decisive time for the maximalists. They feel the need to respond to the ways that the surrounding culture, with its puzzling combination of secular materialism and religious celebration, most intrusively impinges on Jews. Knowing that their children experience the allure of Christmas, maximalist educators arm the cultural battlefronts with a complex set of strategies. They will play up the attractiveness of the Jewish "alternative"—Hanukkah and minimize the attraction of Christmas. This may be done by stressing the religious nature of Christmas and hence its foreignness to Jewish beliefs or by stressing the crass materialism that surrounds the holiday and is unworthy of emulation.

By these standards, Don has not adopted a maximalist position for the Temple Akiba school. The students at Temple Akiba are not asked to wear a kippah at school. While given Hebrew names, they are not consistently called by their Hebrew names and do not engage in formal prayer during school time. While the environment is clearly identifiable as Jewish, and Hebrew is visibly in evidence in every classroom, I never once heard a teacher or student talk of the difference between Jews and non-Jews in terms other than "this is what we do and this is what they do." This practice stands in marked contrast to what Schoem and Heilman report in their studies of more maximalist synagogue schools.[8]

Why has Don not chosen a maximalist approach? Is he a minimalist who believes that Jews ought to be integrated into the general culture with only minimal cultural or religious differences preserved? Is he a pragmatist who assumes that only a minimalist position will be acceptable to the population of Temple Akiba? Does he worry—as any maximalist would—about the dangers of rampant assimilation and the possibility that if American Jews do not guard their unique heritage, they will in short time disappear as a distinct and definable group within American society?[9]

These may have been some of the questions that the teachers had in mind at the orientation. They are questions that take us to the heart of the educational philosophy of the school at Temple Akiba.

A Philosophy of Choice

A few months after the orientation, I observed a sociodrama that the high school students at Temple Akiba were staging under Molly's direction for their peers and parents. The topic was dating, and in the sociodrama a boy asks a girl out for a date for the next Friday night. Given my own traditional Jewish upbringing, I found myself automatically expecting that one of the rabbis present would remind everyone that Friday night is Shabbat and that they should be coming to services, not going out on dates. But no such statement was forthcoming.

By this point in the fieldwork, I realized my expectation had its roots in my history, not in their educational approach. I had grown up with a Judaism that had clear rules about what one is allowed and not allowed to do on Shabbat. Even after I left the world of Orthodoxy and worked in schools and summer camps affiliated with the Conservative movement, there remained a general understanding that whatever one's own level of religious observance, public behavior was guided by the normative expectations of traditional Judaism; even in the context of a sociodrama, no one publicly asked a fellow Jew out for a Friday night date.

Don helped his teachers to understand how the Temple Akiba approach is different from the traditional one when in the orientation he explained that contemporary Reform Judaism relates to mitzvot as "an option-oriented system" rather than as "divine commandments." In conversation he once explained that he believes that modern Jews face a choice between two fundamental approaches to their Judaism. They may view Judaism in traditional terms as a normative system that God commands and that each Jew is obligated to observe in all its detail. Or they may view it in liberal terms as a resource of traditions that should be studied and understood so that individuals may make informed choices as to what and how to observe.

The educational approach at Temple Akiba is to respect the integrity of the choices people make as individuals and as families. The leadership will encourage even marginal Jews to join so that there is some chance of drawing them into Jewish life. These families will be encouraged to send their children to the most intensive form of Jewish education available at the temple to develop a serious attitude toward Judaism. But there is an understanding that each family sets its own standards of religious observance. If celebrating Christmas is their choice, they expect, and the rabbis agree, that that choice will be respected. No one will tell them, or imply to their children, that they do not belong in the synagogue because there has been an intermarriage in the family or a Christmas tree is decorated each December. There is minimal judgment passed on members' religious behavior.

This respect for the family's choice leads Don to insist that the teachers "view all the children in the school as Jews because that is how they view themselves." When a family decides to send their children to the synagogue school and to participate in temple life, even when some members of the family are not formally Jewish, they are viewed as choosing to live a Jewish life. Given that many Jewish families in this city and across the country have never chosen to join a synagogue or to provide their children with a sustained Jewish education, the rabbis wish to acknowledge and celebrate this choice and commitment. For a teacher to call into question the child's or family's Jewish identity because there are non-Jews in the home who celebrate their holidays, in the view of the rabbis, shows disrespect for the Jewish choices the family has made.

In this second regard, the approach is minimalist. At Temple Akiba a minimal distinction is drawn between people who were born into or formally converted to Judaism and those who are part of a Jewish family and have chosen to be active in the synagogue even though they have never formally converted to Judaism. Although the line between Judaism and Christianity as religions is clearly drawn, the distinction between who is a Jew and who is not is less clearly made than in maximalist congregations.[10]

Maximalist educators bemoan the pace of Jewish assimilation into American culture, but the Temple Akiba clergy take a different approach. In an interview, Rabbi Davidman said that given the tremendous temptations that Jews face to assimilate into American culture, "it's kind of unbelievable that we have preserved as much *Yiddishkeit* as we have." In his view, the educational task of the synagogue is not to fight assimilation, but "to make Jews"—to positively contribute to people's self-identification as Jews. With this view, one does not blame Jews for the religious practices they or their parents have abandoned; instead, one works through modeling and positive reinforcement on drawing them more fully into the community of committed Jews.

At Temple Akiba Judaism is presented, as noted in Chapter 2, as a serious and complex tradition that needs to be studied carefully so that one may arrive at one's own position as a Jew. The basic assumption is that one's position as a Jew is not dictated by tradition, but arrived at by the study of traditional texts, experimentation with traditional forms, and knowledge of oneself in the contemporary world. In polar contrast to the leadership in yeshivot, the Temple Akiba leadership assumes its members are at home in secular American culture and that they come to learn how to locate themselves as Jews within that culture. The educational approach is fully integrationist: the ideal is to live as a fully committed American Jew, who draws much sustenance and guidance in secular life from ongoing practice and study of the traditions of Judaism.

But the respect for choice and the welcoming of diversity represent only half of the educational approach at Temple Akiba. Alongside this minimalist approach stands a maximalist commitment to serious Jewish education. The leadership believes that successfully opening up the temple and school to a more diverse clientele requires a greater—not lesser—emphasis on the study of Hebrew and traditional Judaism. If Temple Akiba is attracting members who are marginal in their Judaism, the educators feel a deep commitment to teach them and their children a Judaism rich enough in tradition to have a strong chance of touching their lives.

There is a paradoxical quality to this dual approach. It is minimalist on issues of separation but maximalist—in a Reform Jewish context—on issues of Judaic knowledge and practice. The logic behind this duality is that effectively attracting a diversity of Jews to this congregation requires a strong center to draw them in. People on the periphery are attracted by a clear vision of what they may not currently have in their lives: a link with a spiritual tradition.

Simultaneously holding a minimalist and maximalist position generates definite tensions. We observed these

tensions in the family education program when Don's presentation of the traditional view of mourning came into
sharp conflict with contemporary secular notions of the
definition of family. These same tensions are alive in the
classrooms.

Practicing a philosophy of religious choice presents a
unique educational challenge, for the educators are not
preaching to the converted or filling informational gaps for
the committed. Rather, they are presenting Judaism to a
population that is not always certain about its own identity. The very lack of a clear identity impels these educators
to provide extra structure in learning and many opportunities for the students to grapple with a core of tradition that
Judaism represents.

Although Don has no interest in fighting *against*
Christmas—an approach he believes only reinforces the
negative experiences of Hebrew school—he realizes that
children and adults can choose a Jewish alternative only if
they come to understand Judaism in its own terms.
Enabling children and adults to reach this understanding
requires an emphasis on teaching the Hebrew language
and the original texts of the Bible. It means doing all he can
to get the children to come to this school three days a week
so that they stay involved even after reaching Bar or Bat
Mitzvah and participate in the informal youth program as
well as in the school.

Together with Norman Davidman and Rachel Abeles,
Don believes that serious choice needs to be informed
choice. One can only become informed by having been
meaningfully involved in the study of tradition. But meaningful involvement in the study of a traditional religious
culture raises questions for the students and teachers—
questions that surfaced in classroom interactions that I
observed.

Before moving to a close look at classroom learning, it
would be helpful to provide additional background on the
school context by examining the educational leadership
provided by Rabbi Marcus, the structure of the school, and
the relationship between *religious* and *Hebrew* education.

The Marcus Leadership

Don Marcus was both the clear leader of the Temple Akiba school and the primary informant for this part of my study. We had known each other only distantly before this study, but in a short time developed a close working relationship. We had much in common and found in one another a sympathetic audience for our mutual concerns about Jewish education.

As ethnographer, I also needed to gain some distance, to see Don not only as a partner in my research, but also as the rabbi who served as temple educator in this synagogue. I did this by observing him at many different moments in his work and by speaking to a variety of people on his staff and in the synagogue who shared their perspectives on Don as rabbi and educator.

To understand Don's leadership of the temple school, I wanted to begin with the question of why he made the move from the pulpit to the school. It is unusual in the career of a rabbi to begin as a congregational rabbi and voluntarily move within the same synagogue to assume the leadership of the educational program. I heard Don tell the teachers that he never intended to become a head of a temple school, and in an interview he admitted that his colleagues outside Temple Akiba greeted his decision with puzzlement. In their view, why would a talented and aspiring young rabbi voluntarily settle for what at best could be considered a parallel career move?[11]

My curiosity led me to research the move. The research led back to the 1970s, in the years immediately before Norman and Don arrived at Temple Akiba. At that time the school was presided over by its veteran principal, Fred Robbins.

By profession a public school educator, Fred had led the school during its heyday in the 1950s and 1960s when the school's reputation and the postwar baby boom had kept enrollments high—at over one thousand. The lore about the school in those days was that it provided one of the finest Reform Jewish educational experiences of its time and was the pride of the congregation. Some of the teachers had national reputations within the Reform movement for their excellence.

Yet during the 1970s, the school, as part of the congregation, faced a decline. The baby boomers had already graduated and enrollments began a downward spiral. Beyond the numbers was the sense, expressed by one parent in a retrospective interview, that the mode of education offered was not meeting the needs of a next generation:

> The school was then very formal and lifeless. There was no music, no art, etc. The numbers of students had dropped substantially from the heyday. . . . I and a friend got very involved in the PTA. . . . In 1974 the new addition to the temple opened, and the temple was planning a dedication. The plans did not include a role for families and children. I said the PTA wanted the children present and proposed a day for families and children. There was resistance from the top, but the plan was okayed. Well, 1,500 people showed up, and that sent a message.

The congregation still seemed to be living in the era when young people were to be seen but not heard. Yet to attract a next generation of young members—and that was a priority for this aging congregation—this old-fashioned style would have to be modified. A number of steps were taken to attract younger families to the temple. Among those was a decision to change the direction of the school and search for a new principal to lead the process of change.

The transition was very painful, according to a veteran teacher. The search committee failed to come up with attractive candidates to become educational director. Nevertheless, one candidate was selected, but soon he did not work out. One of the veteran teachers stepped into the role and for the next few years ran the school.

In 1978 Norman Davidman and Don Marcus arrived, committed to embarking on a new chapter in the life of the congregation and its educational programs. Don became very involved with the informal youth program and outreach to different populations. The rabbis began welcoming children and families into the services and programs of the congregation, and the culture of the temple began to change. In 1981, when the veteran teacher-principal decided to retire, Don had not yet thought of stepping into that role, and the congregation hired a third rabbi, Ken Davis, to be the temple's educational director.

The new educational director lasted for only two years. One of the current coordinators explained why:

> Ken Davis posted office hours. He wanted to run it as a school. Even before him it had been looser and there was a closer connection to the temple. Ken was into curriculum development, but a good educational director has to be in tune with people's needs.

When Rabbi Davis left in 1983, the post of temple educator had not been successfully filled since Fred Robbins left in the mid-1970s. The enrollment in religious school had fallen to around three hundred children, and the rabbis' dreams for initiating a new era in the congregation's educational life had yet to be realized.

Don Marcus' move into that position was surely related to his personal closeness to Norman Davidman and their strong sense of sharing a vision. Wondering who initiated the move, I asked Norman, who insisted the initiative had come from Don. When I asked Don, he affirmed that it had been his own suggestion, "a tentative service to Temple Akiba before moving on to a next position."

What began as tentative has lasted over time. By the year of my fieldwork, Don was in his eighth year as temple educator. Don has never entirely relinquished his pulpit role; he is a rabbi in the congregation, a very active part of the clergy team, and preaches on the High Holidays and leads other services and programs. Yet his primary role has been as temple educator, a position he candidly admits lacks the prestige of the pulpit. He plans to return to the pulpit,[12] but in these years has devoted himself to bringing to reality a vision for the school and congregation that he and Norman share.

How did Don make the transition from pulpit rabbi to educator? I asked each of the veteran coordinators to describe that process.

> *Ruth: Because he was a pulpit rabbi coming the other way to education, he felt in the early years that he did not have the expertise. I had been in education and therefore could be of help to him. He was very open to that.*
>
> *Molly: Don had a key to the organization of the temple that others wouldn't have. . . . He was very involved with people . . . and runs the school by getting good faculty. As a "people person," he knows how to get good people.*

Don brought to this position two strengths that were very much in evidence during the year of this study. He is comfortable in hiring good people and allowing them autonomy along with his support. Second, he knows his way around the temple organization and how to harness congregational resources for educational purposes.

His creation of the position of the coordinators illustrates both these strengths. As Ruth indicates, it must have been a daunting task for a rabbi new to formal education to assume responsibility for supervising the teachers and developing the curriculum. Don did not try the impossible, but chose to seek funding for this middle-level position which is often missing in synagogue schools. These head teachers are each highly experienced in a particular area—early childhood, preadolescence, and Hebrew instruction—and lend to the school not only a needed supervisory capacity, but also a curricular expertise. I know of no other synagogue school in this area that has developed a comparable system, but Don conceived the idea and sold it to the temple board.

He convinced the board of two other key ideas that have greatly influenced the school under his leadership. The first relates to teacher salaries and the second to the integration of the high school and youth programs.

As the core of experienced teachers from the previous era began retiring, Temple Akiba faced a new challenge in hiring teachers. There was no longer the pool of veterans devoted to this temple; instead there was open competition with all other area synagogues for the best available teachers. Don realized he needed to spread a wide net and to offer good support and working conditions, but in the end, money also mattered. He went to the board—during the prosperous mid-1980s—with the proposition that essential to quality education was a quality staff. To hire that kind of staff would require a substantial boost in salary. He won an increase of 30 percent in the salary for each teaching position. That placed Temple Akiba in the forefront of teaching salaries in the area.

From his earlier experience with the temple youth program, Don noticed that "commonly kids love youth group and hate high school." So he devised a solution.

> Typically congregations hire two separate staffs. The kids end up having contact with only part-time staff who have no real attachment to the synagogue. The kids graduate and the staff leave. Then the source of attachment is gone.

Knowing that separating formal from informal education is ineffective for adolescents, Don asked why the temple had been hiring two different part-time staffs for the high school and youth group. The answer was organizational: two different lay committees supervised the two domains. But those lay groups could be brought together and shown why a common hiring would work better. Don used his knowledge of congregational organization to create a solution that everyone could accept. There is now more overlap between the domains and a more full-time youth director who also teaches in the high school. Further, the synchrony between formal and informal education extends down in age into the religious school, where children are offered a number of informal opportunities for involvement each year well before their becoming Bar or Bat Mitzvah.

Central to Don's educational thinking is the assumption that staff ought to function as anchors of attachment for the children. David Schoem has written that the synagogue school functions as a part-time institution with all the built-in limitations (pp. 68–70). Don knows that to be true but wants to counter its emotionally numbing effects by building into the experience some lasting contacts between children and adults. Each of his proposed structural changes also works to create an emotionally cohesive environment. Teachers who are paid more can be asked to spend more time preparing for class, getting to know their children, and reflecting on their teaching practice. The coordinators are available to follow the children from grade to grade as well as to work closely with the teachers on their classroom skills and mastery of curriculum. A more full-time youth director has the time to form connections to the temple's adolescents and to plug the youth program into the rhythms of temple life. Finally, there are the clergy who teach during the junior high school years, participate in the Bar or Bat Mitzvah, and teach again in the high school years. They, most of all, represent continuity and a connection between schooling and life-cycle experience.

Don Marcus has learned to function as both rabbi and educator. As rabbi he self-consciously symbolizes the connection between the synagogue's religious and educational programs. He also takes a pastoral attitude toward the parents of the school. He reaches out and offers his time and attention to help them not only with school-related issues, but also with their own search to lead a Jewish life. They relate to him with that special respect that the title "Rabbi" can carry.

As educator Don functions as the connector between the school and the temple. He assures that the school's agenda gets a fair hearing before the board and that the school's interests are protected when the board is doing its business. He does this in conjunction with the other clergy and the religious school committee.[13]

In a large synagogue like Temple Akiba, there are many lay committees, and some function better than others. Often the school committee—with its lay responsibility to set policy for the school and to represent the school in the temple's annual budget deliberations—is not a very powerful group within the temple polity. Don, however, has spent much time and effort in developing a school committee that is very committed to reviewing the school program and in representing the school well in the congregational polity.

As educator Don also has been active in working as a link between the synagogue and federation communities. The Jewish federation in this city has become increasingly involved in matters of Jewish education, and its leaders have often looked to Don to work with them on developing community-wide policies concerning Jewish education. He has been called on to represent the Reform perspective and to work on issues like bolstering communal assistance to synagogue education and providing financial incentives for youth to travel to Israel.

Finally, as educator Don has supervised the school's adoption of a most ambitious and intellectually demanding Hebrew curriculum. This curriculum, developed by the Melton Research Center of the Jewish Theological Seminary of America, was first selected by Ken Davis. Don decided to maintain the program and invest in training the teachers to deliver the curriculum effectively. The hiring of the Hebrew coordinator is directly linked to the complexity of this task. Don shares with Norman Davidman the belief that giving the children the ability to read and understand classical Hebrew texts is essential to the goals of the educational program.

Under Don's leadership the school has grown. From a low point in enrollment of 282 children in 1984/85, the religious school registered 400 students in 1989/90. Don points out this increase has taken place while the synagogue schools in close vicinity continued to lose enrollment.[14] He believes families are choosing the Temple Akiba school because of the quality of its educational programs and its outreach and welcome to a diverse Jewish population.

The education budget has also increased under his leadership. During 1984/85 this budget totaled almost $239,000; five years later it had expanded to $402,000. While the student body also grew, the per-capita expenditure for each student increased from $624 to $884. The education budget rose from 22 to 27 percent of the temple's total operating budget in these five years. The single largest increase was for teachers' salaries, which stood at $76,000 and rose to $190,000. Even given a larger faculty, that constitutes a substantial increase in average salary and reflects the congregational resolve to allow Don the financial means to hire a quality staff to operate the temple's educational program.[15]

The Structure of the School

The Temple Akiba school has a complex structure. It is made up of three programs: the religious school on Sunday, the Hebrew program on Tuesday and Thursday afternoons, and the high school on Monday evenings. This year the school's total population in kindergarten through twelfth grade was 457 students.

First organized in 1912, the Sunday religious school is the oldest and largest of the programs. Currently, the religious school includes three populations:

(1) 123 children in kindergarten through second grade who come only on Sunday;
(2) 208 students in grades three to seven who come on Sunday and during the week; and,
(3) 36 students from grades three to eight who come only on Sunday.

The religious school is structured so that the three youngest grades meet only once a week as an introduction to Jewish education and as a preparation for the more intensive program of Sunday plus midweek Hebrew that begins in third grade. However, until the religious school committee changed this policy (a change described in Chapter 5), families at the end of second grade could choose to continue in a Sunday-only program. In this option, a continuation of the classical Reform model, the child receives primarily an English-based religious education with only a minimal exposure to the Hebrew language. This option does not lead to Bar or Bat Mitzvah, for the Hebrew knowledge needed for the Bar Mitzvah ceremony is not provided. But it does allow the child to continue on to the high school and be eligible for the confirmation ceremony that is held after tenth grade. Twenty-five students have currently chosen this option.

With kindergarten through grade eight in attendance on Sunday morning—a total of twenty-one classes—the school building is in full use. The morning begins at 9:45 and runs until 12:15. It is divided into three forty-five-minute periods. The younger grades stay in one classroom for the morning, although their activities vary. The older grades have homeroom plus three distinct classes, usually with different teachers.

The Sunday staffing is also very full. Besides the teachers for the twenty-one classes, there are also the three coordinators, the clergy who teach grades seven and eight, the art, music, and audiovisual specialists, the special needs teacher, and the Hebrew specialists who help with Hebrew instruction. In total there are thirty-four staff members for the religious school.

This large number of staff reflects the complex agenda of the religious school. As many of the regular teachers are new to the school and to teaching, the coordinators are present to both observe the teaching and meet with the teachers after children leave. Staff meetings, for which teachers are paid extra, take place regularly, and teachers are expected to attend at 12:15 on Sunday. These are opportunities to review classroom work as well as to plan the curriculum for coming weeks.

Hebrew is taught for one period on Sunday. As many of the regular teachers are not trained in language instruction, the Hebrew specialists—who are from the midweek Hebrew program—teach the more advanced classes in grades three to six. All classes, but especially those in the lower grades, are introduced to Hebrew and Jewish culture through music, art, and audiovisual displays. Having specialists in these areas—as well as specialists who work with students with special needs—gives Temple Akiba a range of possibilities that is unusual for a synagogue school.

The Hebrew program that meets for two afternoons during the week is designed for grades three to seven. It functions as a preparation for Bar or Bat Mitzvah even though the curriculum followed has much broader goals than the Bar or Bat Mitzvah itself. Students attend on Tuesday and Thursday afternoons from 4:00 to 5:30 P.M. after having attended their public or private school. They have one teacher for the three hours of Hebrew, most of which is devoted to the Melton curriculum in classical Hebrew. The teachers, however, do vary the learning experience and include a variety of topics: Jewish holidays, customs, values, and Israel.

The Hebrew program is distinct from the Sunday religious school. The midweek program has its own faculty and curriculum, and although half of these teachers also teach on Sunday, the two programs have a different character; the midweek program is a more structured and intensive learning experience. Although on Sunday students of this age move from class to class and experience to experience, during the week they are solely focused on learning Hebrew and Judaica. Also while there were only twenty-seven Sunday sessions held during the year, there were sixty-two sessions held during the week. This discrepancy has to do with when the Jewish holidays fall but also reflects the school's scheduling policy that whenever there is a three-day weekend, Sunday school is not held.

Every entering student begins in the religious school; attending the midweek Hebrew program has been highly encouraged, but voluntary. Of the 236 students who attended grades three to seven on Sundays, 110 attended the midweek Hebrew program. They were divided among ten classes that averaged eleven students per class. Don has justified this class size (Sunday classes in these grades ranged from seventeen to twenty-seven students with a mean of twenty) on the grounds that second-language instruction offered late in the afternoon requires smaller groupings and student/teacher ratios. The smaller class size contributes to the program's different atmosphere.

Of the 126 students who were not in the Hebrew midweek program, 84 were in a Hebrew tutorial program. As described in the parent handbook, the tutorial program

> has been designed for students who are unable
> to attend our Hebrew school program. It is a pro-
> gram of individualized instruction . . . 30 hours of
> tutorial instruction during the year. . . . The focus
> and goal is to bring students to a level of Hebrew
> which will enable them to prepare for Bar or Bat
> Mitzvah. The level of integration between Hebrew
> and other areas of Jewish study is much lower than
> it is in the Hebrew school program. . . .

The tutorial program is a response to the fact that Temple Akiba draws families from a wide metropolitan area and that some people live far enough away that getting into the city twice during the week would be very difficult. In addition, some students attend private schools that have compulsory after-school programs that conflict with the regular Hebrew program. With Hebrew instruction compulsory for becoming Bar or Bat Mitzvah, the school felt it needed to develop this alternative to the regular Hebrew program.

Yet, unlike the other programs for which no tuition is paid,[16] the tutorial program is paid for directly by parents. It costs $950 to hire a Hebrew tutor for one child. The money is paid to the temple, and the Hebrew coordinator selects the tutor for the child. Some tutors are the school's teachers, who are making extra money, but many are hired especially for tutoring. The coordinator keeps in touch with all the tutors to insure that the Melton curriculum is being taught properly and that the students are learning. In spite of the extra cost, the tutorial program is popular, as the numbers indicate.

There are also two Hebrew classes during the week for students with special learning needs. These, which do not cost parents extra money, reflect the temple's commitment to serve this population. These 17 students bring the total number of students studying Hebrew during the week to 211. For the 25 students who have chosen the Sunday-only option, Hebrew instruction is limited to one period on Sunday morning.

The Monday-night high school program is designed to be distinct from the other two school programs. Recognizing the adolescent's wish to be treated differently, Don and the staff have created a program that is elective in nature and more actively mixes formal and informal educational formats.

Students arrive at 5:30 P.M. on Monday for an informal dinner with their peers and the faculty. At 6:30 the first of two one-hour classes begins. The courses are designed for one of three levels—eighth, ninth to tenth, and eleventh to twelfth grades—and each runs for seven or fourteen weeks. The courses thus alternate several times during the year. They are taught by the clergy, the youth director, and three other teachers. An elective modern Hebrew course is offered to the eighth grade. All other courses are in English and range in subject from Jewish practice to ethics to comparative religion.

Two particularly interesting courses are offered by Don Marcus and Molly Siegel. Don teaches a course to the older students in modern Jewish theology that features not only learning about the thinkers, but also constructing a theology of one's own out of the elements of existing theologies. Molly directs a course on improvisational drama that focuses on issues of Jewish family life. The course is open to all high school students and also attracts a few parent participants. The group works all semester to prepare a presentation for fellow students and their parents. These never fail to draw a crowd or to stir debate as the topics touch home. The three presentations I observed dealt with how to choose a college, what input parents should have in their children's dating decisions, and how the Gulf War polarized opinion in families of this liberal Jewish community.

There were ninety students attending the high school: twenty-eight in eighth, twenty-eight in ninth, fifteen in tenth, and nineteen in the combined eleventh and twelfth grades. Don told how hard it is in this geographically spread-out congregation to build a community among students who attend seventy-four different public and private schools, often come to and go from temple by car pool, and rarely have the opportunity to "hang around" and get to know one another. The staff invest a good deal of effort in using informal activities to create a sense of a group. The effort seems to have paid off as more students are choosing to return after their Bar or Bat Mitzvah for both classes and youth activity.[17]

Confirmation, the classical Reform ceremony for welcoming a group of tenth-grade students into the adult community, retains importance in the life of the high school and temple. Each year the members of the tenth grade go away with the staff early in September for the confirmation *kallah,* or convocation. This experience is intended to help consolidate the group and build the relation between the group and the staff. They devote much time in May of that year to preparing a service and program that takes place on Shavuot. As a group they make their statement to the congregation, who symbolically confirms their place in the adult community on the holiday that celebrates the original receiving of the Torah.

"Religious" and "Hebrew" Education

The division in the elementary grades between the two programs—the Sunday religious school and the midweek Hebrew program—is rooted in the history of Temple Akiba, but it continues to reflect the somewhat divided views within the congregation of what constitutes a Jewish education. I will begin with some observations of the religious school in action.

It is a beautiful Sunday morning in April several days after the Passover holiday. Religious school at Temple Akiba is in session after a week's recess for Passover and before a two-week recess for spring vacation in the local public schools. Discontinuity is clearly an issue today, but also on the agenda is an Israel fair to which families are invited immediately after school.

At 10:00 o'clock Paula Lieberman stands before twelve seventh-graders in a course on Israel. Paula, a master's student in science education, is new to the school this year and came on the recommendation of a friend who taught here last year. She teaches only on Sundays and confides later that it has not been easy to engage the attention of her seventh-graders. Also, the curriculum for the Israel course has been under revision.

Today she is dividing the students into six pairs—each of whom is to prepare a short skit on a famous tourist spot in Israel. The pairs go off with an information sheet on their location and are to return within twenty minutes with their dramatic presentation. I recognize here the influence of Molly—the coordinator for this grade—who loves to inject drama into the life of the classroom.

The students work independently and in an orderly fashion—some in the classroom and some out in the hall. Within twenty minutes the first pair of boys are ready. Paula asks them to wait quietly for the others. It takes about ten more minutes until all are ready with their skits.

With everyone back in their seats, the first pair present on Masada, the mountaintop fortress built in the Judean desert during the first century as part of the Jewish zealots' struggle against Roman rule. One boy plays Caesar; the other plays the messenger from the war front, and then the oracle.

> *Ceasar: Report on the zealots!*
> *Messenger: One thing: all the Jews are dead.*
> *Caesar: What?*
> *Messenger: They didn't want to be slaves. It's against their religion.*
> *Caesar: Bring in the oracle! What do you see as the future of this spot?*
> *Oracle: In the future I see a tourist trap. It still belongs to the Jews.*
> *Caesar: Throw him to the lions!*

The other students applaud and Paula quickly asks: What year? They answer "Seventy." The second Temple in Jerusalem was destroyed by the Romans in 70 C.E. and Masada fell three years later, but Paula lets the answer stand. She next asks: How did they die? "They killed themselves." She does not have the time to pursue why they would kill themselves or whether their religion compelled that decision. Paula thanks them and is on to the next skit on the *Kotel,* or Wailing Wall, in Jerusalem.

Before the forty-five-minute period is up, all six skits are presented. It is a series of rushed performances of mixed quality. Some are clever, some dull, but all are informative. There is no question that these students know how to organize information and present it coherently. The variation is in the level of creativity and drama. The class responds enthusiastically to some and sits in bored silence through others.

After the bell rings, Paula hands back written work they have done and quickly mentions a film they saw about the West Bank. But time is up, and she is a bit frustrated by the clock. Walking down to the lounge, she offers her view on teaching in the religious school.

> This is a nice place to teach, but once a week isn't much. By seventh grade the main objective is to get the kids to feel good about being Jewish, and there isn't that much opportunity for learning. There are many interruptions for vacations and even when school is in session. In class I have to keep things moving so they will do the work. In my first semester here I gave homework and tests. But I found out that is not the Temple Akiba way. Now I am using making a video as a way of organizing.

The frustration with the once-a-week format is not Paula's alone. It is shared by Don Marcus and the religious school committee and is one reason they have pushed to have the students enroll for the midweek Hebrew program. Yet generations of teachers have learned to teach under these conditions and Paula is now learning as well.

While homework assignments are common in the Hebrew program, they are less common on Sunday, when the focus is more experiential—on what takes place in the class itself. The suggestion to make a video in class came from Molly and represents her sense that active learning works best in this context. Clearly, formal testing is not in place on Sunday.

Paula senses that seventh grade is a turning point in this school. It is the year of the Bar or Bat Mitzvah, and students are working with the cantor and a tutor to prepare their Bar or Bat Mitzvah portions; that sometimes takes them out of class. It is also the year that they begin studying the Torah with one of the rabbis on Sunday mornings. Finally, as the last year before Bar or Bat Mitzvah, seventh grade is when the school tries to attract the students to continue their Jewish education into adolescence. There are more informal activities planned for this year to draw them into the temple community. These include weekends away with the youth group and, twice a year, attendance at the high school's drama presentations. These extras cut into regular class time on Sunday.

When Don and I met to discuss areas of focus for my research, he suggested the seventh grade as a focus since it is the year when school and synagogue functions come into greatest synchrony. Bar and Bat Mitzvah preparation leads the way, but the study with the clergy and the intensified informal education are also part of the designed synchrony. My previous research on seventh-graders from an Israeli kibbutz made me receptive, although in the end the focus expanded to grades seven through nine.

Paula's class typified much of what I had observed in the religious school. A number of experienced teachers teach with more skill, assurance, and intellectual acuity than was evident in Paula's class. But Don observed on several occasions that his greatest single frustration as a principal is the turnover in young, inexperienced teachers in the religious school. Typically, they come to teach after graduating college, get some initial training from the coordinator, and then leave after a year or two when their life circumstances change. Paula evidenced openness to Molly's supervision and was learning to teach under these difficult conditions. But how long would she remain?

The struggle with finding sufficient time is also common. It takes longer to organize a class in which students are involved in active learning. By the time the pairs had prepared their skits, thirty minutes had elapsed and there remained only fifteen minutes for all six presentations. No wonder the pace of presentation was rushed and there was no time to either explore interesting questions—such as why the defenders of Masada would have committed mass suicide—or to conclude the lesson with an appropriate summary of the learning. The discontinuity inherent in meeting only once a week only exacerbates the sense that learning in these classes often seems fragmented.

Yet even at this trying age, the students remained on task throughout the period. During one of the drier presentations on Israel, when minds could be wandering, the students were not prone to acting out. On the whole, with some clear exceptions, the religious school—like the Hebrew program—is less burdened by the behavioral problems that characterize some other synagogue schools.[18]

Paula's class is part of the religious school curriculum not because the subject is religion, but because the goal of the religious school is to teach the basic knowledge that one needs to know to be an informed participant in today's Jewish world. Among the series of goals listed in the parent handbook is "to recognize Israel as the historic homeland of all Jews and recognize our obligation to preserve Israel for future generations." This goal fits well into what Woocher calls "the civil religion of American Jews," which is in evidence at Temple Akiba not only in the formal curriculum but also in the Israel fair held each spring.[19]

The term "religious school" dates back to the early years of the temple when Reform Judaism maintained a more strictly religious definition of itself. Until the 1940s the educational program of the temple was limited to learning in English about the Bible, holidays, customs, and ethics of Judaism. While all those foci have been maintained, the religious school now introduces both Hebrew language and learning about Israel as early as kindergarten and first grade.

This is not to suggest that Hebrew is viewed as being a secular subject. Quite the opposite. In the parent handbook one reads, "Our Hebrew programs seek to integrate the study of Hebrew language, liturgy, mitzvot and Jewish thought in a graded five-year curriculum. . . . Familiarity with the Hebrew language enables students to attain a richer understanding of themselves as Jews . . . and a link with Jews throughout the world." Hebrew is being taught less for purposes of ordering a falafel in Tel Aviv than for reading Genesis and praying the *Sh'ma* in the original.

This choice to teach classical Hebrew[20] and invest heavily in the training and supervision of Hebrew teachers[21] is an expression of the value that Rabbis David-man and Marcus have placed on the study of traditional Jewish texts as an anchor for the "Torah" they are teaching this congregation. They make no actual distinction between religious and Hebrew studies, but consider both integral to their definition of Jewish education. While some congregants are still loyal to an older concept of religious education, Rabbi Marcus has worked to bring the temple leadership to a newer vision in which religious and Hebrew education are integrated on the formal side and linked to the informal educational programs to form a comprehensive package of Jewish education.

Don realistically knows the limits of what can be accomplished educationally within the framework of a part-time synagogue school. But he would insist that if the synagogue takes its educational mission seriously and invests in providing a quality education within the limits of the part-time structure, two positive outcomes can be achieved: the students will gain a strong basis for continuing their education as Jews beyond the years of formal schooling, and they and their families will be drawn into a warm and caring Jewish community that will sponsor their Jewish living and growing for as long as they live in this area.

An ethnographic study is not designed to test rigorously the validity of Rabbi Marcus' claims. But the next chapter will take a close look at teaching and learning in the Temple Akiba school to clarify the cultural dynamics of Jewish learning within the classroom setting.

Chapter 4

A Close Look at Classroom Learning

After examining the philosophy of education that guides the work of the Temple Akiba educators and the structure that organizes their teaching within the school, we turn in this chapter to the next question: What makes it challenging for teachers to teach and students to learn in the context of this synagogue school?

An assumption underlies this second question, and it arises from the previous literature on supplementary Jewish education. It is that presenting the traditions of Judaism to modern American Jews—children or adults—is a culturally complex task, for there is no easy match between the basic tenets of traditional Judaism and the worldview of most American Jews.

In turning to consider the detailed interactions among teachers and students in the classes of this school, I have found this assumption helpful in organizing the observations. In looking at these classes, I have asked myself: How do the teachers and students handle the dissonance that arises between their modern—and, I must add, secular—perspectives on the world and the conceptual frameworks that characterize traditional religious texts and practices? In the classroom it is usually the teachers who take on the role of presenting the traditional text or practice and the students who react from the modernist perspective. But my primary interest has been in seeing how they work together to make possible a lively dialogue between tradition and modernity. For what has most fascinated me in observing these classroom interactions is how, for all they protest against traditional concepts, many of the students

102 Succeeding at Jewish Education

are invested in the dialogue and keep the conversation going among themselves and with their teachers.

In this chapter, the detailed observations of the learning and teaching that takes place in the classrooms will focus on the upper grades of the school and on the centerpiece of the Temple Akiba curriculum: the study of the biblical text.

Virtually all synagogue schools teach the Torah, but not many place the central emphasis that this school does on the close study of the text. The students begin studying the Hebrew Bible from the early grades. At first they learn the stories, then parts of the Bible through an edited edition; only in seventh grade do they open an actual Bible and begin their "face-to-face" encounter with the text.[1]

Students at Temple Akiba acquire the competencies for engaging in close textual study in the religious school and Hebrew program where, as we have seen, much of the learning is a preparation for the encounter with the biblical text. The culminating point for the religious school curriculum are the classes that the rabbis teach in seventh and eighth grades that involve a close reading of the biblical text. Rabbi Davidman teaches Genesis to the seventh-graders and Rabbi Abeles teaches Exodus to the eighth-graders.

In an interview, Rabbi Davidman explained that while rabbis in many other congregations prefer to teach the students only during their high school years, he has chosen to begin teaching them during seventh grade as a way of helping to influence their choice to continue studying after their Bar or Bat Mitzvah. Perhaps he also wants the first connection between rabbi and child not to be in the very public encounter of the Bar Mitzvah ceremony, but in the more everyday context of the classroom. Significantly, he and Rabbi Abeles have chosen studying the biblical text as the basis for their first connection to these young adolescents.

Given this emphasis in the curriculum, it is appropriate to ask, What is the nature of text study in the school? I observed classes of both rabbis teaching in the religious school as well as several seventh-grade Bible classes in the

Hebrew program. While no one class is representative, I have chosen to review two in detail: Rabbi Abeles teaching Exodus to the eighth-graders and Barbara Zimmerman, a Hebrew teacher, teaching Jonah to the seventh grade. These classes are illustrative of the styles of teaching found in the upper grades, the kinds of learning that the older students engage in, and the tensions that arise in these classes when these contemporary students and teachers join together in trying to make sense of traditional texts.

In presenting these classes, I am following the lead of Samuel Heilman, who, in his ethnographies of Jewish study, highlights two aspects of the dynamics that are relevant here.[2] First, these classes are occasions for the public expression and performance of students' and teachers' identities as Jews. Neither students nor teachers are "simply" learning the text; rather they are approaching this group learning as an opportunity to give voice to their own understandings of themselves and others as Jews. Second, in so approaching the text, the students experience some cultural and cognitive dissonance between their view of themselves as modern Americans and what the text in its narrative expresses as a Jewish worldview. Together the teachers and students find themselves dealing with the dissonance and trying to cope with the realization that there is no easy synchrony between tradition and modernity.

Teaching Exodus

Rabbi Rachel Abeles teaches the eighth grade during the third and last period on Sunday. This particular class took place on the same Sunday morning after Passover as Paula's class on Israel.

Rachel begins the class by asking the four girls and five boys assembled about their Passover seders. Tamar reports that at her family seder they used "old, traditional haggadahs," but the "women outnumbered the men" so the seder was "real feminist." Daniel tells of an "old friend of the family" who came to their seder, a "sixty-four-year-old Polish Jew, survivor of the [concentration] camps" who was "not as traditional as you'd think."

In these reports one already hears the theme of tradition and modernity. The haggadot were traditional and old, but the seder was feminist and hence modern. The friend of the family was from the old world of Poland, but not as traditional in his religious observance as you'd think. The students seem to be balancing the categories of "old" and "new" in their attempts to describe their Jewish experience.

Turning to Exodus, Rachel asks Daniel to report on a conversation he had with his father after the last class about "his disillusionment with the God in Exodus." Daniel reports:

> Two weeks ago we read in Exodus that God tells Moses to tell Pharaoh to let the Jews go. But God said, "I'll harden his heart." God set Pharaoh up. God is a murderer too because He killed all the Egyptian firstborn.

Daniel is referring to the images in Exodus of God's hardening Pharaoh's heart so that even after several plagues Pharaoh does not set the people of Israel free from their bondage. Daniel sees hardening Pharaoh's heart as God's setting Pharaoh up to be the heartless opponent who God then has to knock down with the remainder of the plagues, including the killing of all the firstborn in Egypt. Daniel calls God a murderer for having "killed all the Egyptian firstborn."

Although Daniel's calling God a murderer might have taken her aback, Rachel responds calmly by asking if the killing of the firstborn Egyptians mirrors anything earlier in the biblical story. Jenny responds:

> It's an act of revenge, an eye for an eye. Pharaoh said to kill all the male firstborn [of the Israelites] and God then killed all the [Egyptian] firstborn. It's not right. It should be "turn the other cheek."

This is said with great adolescent excitement. With

equal force Tamar rises to the defense. "Two hundred years of slavery, the loss of dignity, and the killing of their babies are much more than the [killing of] the firstborn." But Joshua is not convinced:

> Don't confuse God with the king. God is supposed to be righteous. You can't compare God to Pharaoh.
> God did it to prove that He is something. They [the Israelites] had lost their faith.

Joshua and the others are making good use of the detail of the narrative in developing their contrasting arguments, but Joshua is also developing an unusual reading of the story: God is acting in Egypt to restore the faith the Israelites had lost.

Daniel adds to their case against the God of Exodus.

> It was not only the young of the [Egyptian] firstborn who were killed, but the old ones too. It must have been 10 percent of the Egyptian population.

He is accurately reading the text: in the plague against the Egyptian firstborn, God killed the firstborn males of all ages. Daniel is arguing that therefore this act is not comparable to Pharaoh's order to kill the Israelite male infants. While Tamar cannot quite rebut these points, she is not about to give up. "You're only human too. How can you see the reasons for this? You can't say it was set up. Maybe it was predestined and not in God's control." Tamar cannot rationalize God's actions, but can point out to His accusers that they too have only limited vision and cannot know why God acts as He does.

The students are delivering their statements in rapid succession and in highly excited tones. As one speaks, the second raises her hand and the third is commenting in stage whispers on why the logic of the other's statement is faulty. The quality of their arguments is impressive, but there is the possibility that this debate could whirl out of control.

Rachel, who has been mostly witnessing their debate, now steps in to introduce what she had planned for this week: a study of the question, "What was the real reason that God wanted to free the Israelites from Egypt?" The vocal students want to continue their debate, but Rachel is quite insistent that it end. She divides all the students—five of whom have not yet participated in the lesson—into four small groups and gives them the assignment of looking up a printed list of verses from the first twelve chapters of Exodus that will be the basis for their answering the question she has posed.

As the students spend the next ten minutes reviewing the texts and preparing their responses, I ponder Rachel's role in what has taken place. She set the stage for the debate by asking Daniel to recall his thoughts from the previous class. She seemed to be building a bridge from the last session to the present, but she also must have realized that his rather heretical position would elicit strong reaction. Tamar is the one to take up the defense, but Rachel chooses not to take sides. She could have introduced a more traditional reading of God's actions, but I recall from observing her in other contexts that her teaching style is to elicit free expression of opinion and not come on as the defender of the faith.

Rachel is walking around helping the groups of students. She stresses in a more didactic tone that they will need to base their statements on direct citations from the Bible. "In research papers you need footnotes. In Torah you need citations as prooftexts." The students are following her directive in their groups. The ones who were active in the debate are active now. The others are participating in the small groups but are not the leaders.

Daniel and his partner are the first to report:

In Exodus, chapter 2, verse 25 it says: "God looked upon the Israelites, and God took notice of them." God focused on the Israelites and called them "My firstborn son" (4:22). God makes a distinction between them and the Egyptians. Look at chapter

9:1–7. It's making a distinction. They [the Israelities] are different and have to be judged separately.

Rachel asks the class if they understand the report. It is not clear that they do, as the argument is wrapped in verses and does not seem to answer the question posed. Joshua, in a teasing voice, asks his friend, "Where is the eye-opener?" Daniel admits there is no eye-opener, and he and his partner sit down.

Jenny and her partner are next:

> God was afraid that if He left the Israelites in Egypt any longer they would convert and assimilate into Egypt. He could not allow that. Look at Exodus 5:19–23, which says that the people say that we've lost trust in God. It's much easier to follow Pharaoh's gods because God just makes trouble.

Time is now running out. Rachel quickly asks Joshua and his partners to report. Joshua says, "God has a bond to these people. Everyone has a bond with God, but their bond is the strongest. But if God has the strongest bond to them, why does He need to do all this killing?"

As that hardly answers the question posed, Rachel asks: "What is the real reason that God took them out?" Joshua responds: "So they wouldn't lose faith." Rachel hurriedly calls on Tamar and her partner, but before they can begin, the bell rings. As if on cue, the debate resumes.

> *Daniel: The reason God needs to go through all this is that there hasn't been a lot of proof for thousands of years of the existence of God. So we are atheists and they too didn't believe.*
>
> *Joshua: If we were in another culture for a long time, we too wouldn't be Jewish any longer.*
>
> *Jenny: If times are good like now, God doesn't appear. But in times of trouble He does.*

These last speeches are delivered in rapid succession before anyone has yet moved. Having had the last word, the three get up and leave with the others. As Rachel is gathering her materials, I remark that was quite an interactive group. She responds that she cannot teach a frontal lesson in this class because they would struggle with her for control. "They have to be teaching each other for this class to work." I ask about the students who did not actively participate, and Rachel says they "take turns being in and out" and "only one boy is consistently out."

As we walk down the hall, Rachel takes pride in "insisting upon an intellectual standard" in having the students base their reasoning on citations from the text of Exodus. She notes that they were able to cite chapter and verse. I agree: they consistently demonstrated an awareness of the detail of the biblical text. Yet, the lesson as presented by Rachel did not hold together, and the question she posed did not receive an adequate response.

Rachel, like Paula, chose an interactive format and then ran out of time before being able to bring the lesson to its completion. In a once-a-week, forty-five-minute period it is hard to balance the counterdemands of participation and covering the material, and the bell caught Rachel short. Her choice to bridge back to the past lesson and to the students' experience of Passover did not leave very much time for the lesson of the day. There was not the time to use the verses cited to develop possible answers to the question posed.

What this eighth-grade class has in abundance is intellectual engagement. The active eighth-graders place themselves in the biblical story and use the class discussion as a way of expressing and performing their own experiences as Jews in our culture. As Heilman points out, any serious group study of a traditional text involves some mixture of attempting to read the text in its own terms and interpreting the text in light of the readers' contemporary experience. As these readers are early adolescents, it is not surprising that they lean more heavily to contemporizing than to working through the text in its own terms. In Piaget's terms they are intoxicated with their newly developing capacities to play with ideas on a more abstract level.[3] Yet, they do give the text its due by attending to its detail.

What emerges from this class is a reading of Exodus in light of these adolescents' experience. A review of their statements tells us much about the cultural assumptions they bring to the study of text.

1. For Daniel the God of Exodus is a morally ambiguous character. To be God, He has to live up to an ethical standard that is qualitatively different from the standard of Pharaoh. Once God gets into a power struggle with Pharaoh and resorts to hardening Pharaoh's heart and then killing the Egyptian firstborn, He has betrayed the standard that is God's. Then God is little better than an ancient tyrant. As Jenny adds, God should be turning the other cheek, not seeking an eye for an eye.

2. For Joshua the God of Exodus visited these plagues on the Egyptians as a way of proving to the Israelites "that He is something." That adds to the moral ambiguity of the story but also tells us that God had to act because the people were losing their faith in Him. Jenny later adds that had God "left the Israelites in Egypt any longer they would convert and assimilate into Egypt" because "it's much easier to follow Pharaoh's gods."

3. Daniel concludes the class by jumping between biblical times and the present and announcing that God had to do all that killing because the Israelites in their time, as we in our time, have lost faith in God. He had to give some proof of His existence or everyone would become atheists. Making the same jump, Joshua declares that had we been in another culture as long as the Israelites were in Egypt, "we too wouldn't be Jewish any longer."

For these students, the story of the Exodus is not primarily one of the liberation of a slave people from the bondage of Pharaoh's Egypt, but the assimilation of the Israelites into a foreign culture and the loss of their faith and identity. With the exception of Tamar, who argues that the enslavement of the people is the central motif of the story, the others understand the biblical God as being concerned about losing believers and needing to act quickly lest the Israelites completely assimilate into Egyptian culture.

Although the tradition directs the Jewish reader to identify with their ancestors as slaves in the land of Egypt, these students seem to identify with the Israelites not as slaves, but as people who live in Egyptian culture and find "it's much easier to follow Pharaoh's gods." They assume that their ancestors, like themselves, are asking both moral and theological questions about God's existence and are having trouble believing in a God who either gives no sign of His existence or appears on the stage of history as a destructive force in the life of nations.

With more time than religious school allows, Rachel could have taught these bright students more about the traditional Jewish concern with Exodus as a liberation or salvation text. They could have learned to differentiate between their own questions of belief and the weary slaves' survival concerns. But the strength of Rachel's teaching style is that it encourages the students to identify in their own ways with the ancient narrative and to give voice to their perceptions of the dilemma of Jews living in a foreign culture.

Heilman suggests that Jews study the Holy Book together in groups so that they can hear how each person understands the holy. These eighth-graders are very anxious to be heard on these subjects. They have ideas about God, morality, and cultural assimilation that are important to them and that may not find expression in their regular school experience. Their ideas are not always easy for their elders to hear. Yet Rachel's patient listening—so much in contrast to Roth's portrayal of Rabbi Binder's avid defense of the faith against Ozzie's questions—allows for this articulation of worldview that at their age in particular is essential for the formation of identity.

Yet what is lacking in this short class is the voice of the tradition responding to the students' questions. Almost all of the questions they raise about the Exodus text have been raised before and commented on by centuries of commentators. The dialectic between old and new, tradition and modernity, is not fully played out here. In his study of synagogue schools, Heilman has suggested that when contemporary students meet head-on the tradition and its worldview, the tension is greatest between the "old" and the "new."[4] By not having to respond directly to traditional perspectives, except as presented by one of their peers, Daniel, Joshua, and Jenny were freer to express their own identities without having to wrestle much with the moral and intellectual demands that the traditional text places upon them as modern readers.

To see the tension between tradition and modernity being more fully played out, we turn to Barbara's Hebrew class, which is studying the biblical text of Jonah.

Teaching Jonah

On the first Thursday afternoon in February Barbara's seventh-grade Hebrew class is about to begin its study of the Book of Jonah. This will be their initiation into the study of a full biblical text in Hebrew. Jonah was chosen as the starting point, for this short work tells a familiar but engaging story in a clear narrative Hebrew relatively accessible to the beginner.

Several years of studying classical Hebrew have prepared these students for this step. They have been reading short stories that the authors of the curriculum wrote in the literary style of the Bible and have considerable experience reading and grammatically analyzing biblical language, although not directly from the biblical text. Now they have taken off the "training wheels" of the Melton curriculum and are about to make their way through the opening verses of Jonah.

On this day of winter rains, the five of seven students who are present are using looseleaf texts rather than Hebrew Bibles. At Temple Akiba students are given large-print texts that can be written on rather than small-print sacred books. In these editions the students have the Hebrew text, which does not have the English translation, but does have a dictionary of Hebrew terms to help with word comprehension.

Barbara is one of the three veteran teachers teaching

in the Hebrew program. An artist by training, Barbara spent much of her adolescent years living in Israel and still speaks a beautiful Israeli Hebrew. She began teaching here as a way of supporting herself, and, over the years, has become more professionally involved in Jewish education. Yet her training as a teacher has been on-the-job at Temple Akiba where she been teaching the Melton Hebrew curriculum for the last half-dozen years.

Because of my special interest in seventh grade, I observed Barbara teaching several times in both years of my study. This class, which is one of two at the seventh-grade level in the Hebrew program, has been described by several of the staff as perhaps the best in the recent history of the Hebrew program.[5]

Staci begins reading the first sentence of Jonah in Hebrew: "The Word of the Lord came to Jonah son of Amittai."[6] Barbara asks in modern Hebrew, "Who spoke to Jonah?" and "Who is Jonah's father?" She is checking for simple comprehension and Debby and Andrew supply correct single-word answers. Barbara reads the next half-sentence and asks Nancy to translate. Without referring to her dictionary, Nancy translates: "Go at once to Nineveh, that great city, and proclaim judgment upon it."

Debby concludes the second verse in Hebrew, "for their wickedness has come before Me," and starts down the road of a spontaneous translation. She first spots the word *ra*, which she knows means *bad*. Barbara asks, "What then is *ra'atum*?" Debby correctly identifies the suffix as meaning *their* and demonstrates the Melton approach of "breaking down the word" into its component parts. But she is stuck on the word *altah* (gone up or come before).

> *Barbara: You know the word* aliyah. *What does it mean?*
> *Staci: A Torah portion.*
> *Barbara: Where do you go for the Torah portion?*
> *Debby: On the* bimah.
> *Barbara: How do you get there?*
> *Debby: You go up.*
> *Barbara: Yes, and that is* aliyah.

> *Staci: Couldn't you tell us that?*
> *Barbara: I wanted you to figure it out.*

More than helping the students with the meaning of this verb, Barbara is connecting the Hebrew of the Bible to the more familiar Hebrew of synagogue life. She wants them to see the continuity in the language, in which the phrases commonly used in their Bar or Bat Mitzvah preparation have a meaning and history that otherwise would be missed.

Having worked through the translation, the class begins to discuss God's coming to Jonah to send him on this mission.

> *Barbara: Would you answer God if called?*
> *Debby: Do you mean talk to God?*
> *Barbara: Can we talk to God?*
> *Debby: In prayer?*
> *Barbara: Some people think that praying is talking to God. In the Bible when someone hears God's voice, they respond. Abraham is a prime example of that. But Jonah does not respond in that way, and that is a problem in this book.*
> *Debby: Maybe God spoke to him in a dream?*
> *Barbara: Maybe. Where did we read about that before?*
> *Staci: In a story we read last year.*

Barbara's asking about being called by God leaves Debby uncertain how to respond. "Talking to God" is not a common phrase in Temple Akiba even in reference to prayer. Perhaps sensing the dissonance, Barbara switches back to the original frame of talking about Jonah, and Debby can more comfortably participate.

The class continues with the Hebrew reading: "Jonah, however, started out to flee to Tarshish from the Lord's service." In the previous session, the students had done research on the map of the ancient Mediterranean world to identify the geography of the Jonah story. They know that Tarshish is a port city, which they locate in Sicily. Andrew identifies Nineveh as being in ancient Assyria, which today is Iraq. The students realize that Jonah is fleeing in the opposite direction from Nineveh, and they consider that Jonah may be hoping that God will not see him if he heads in this other direction.

They take on the second half of the third verse: "He went down to Joppa and found a ship going to Tarshish. He paid the fare and went aboard to sail with the others to Tarshish, away from the service of the Lord." Debby remembers the Hebrew for *ship* and Nancy the word for *found*. Andrew successfully works on the verb *went down* and identifies Joppa as the port city of Jaffa in Israel. Rebekka puzzles out word by word "to sail with the others to Tarshish, away from the service of the Lord." Her skill in translating without the use of a dictionary is impressive.

With the hard work of translating this complex verse completed, Debby comments: "I don't understand why Jonah did not want to do what God asked."

> *Barbara: What do you think?*
> *Debby: He was afraid they [the people of Nineveh] would kill him.*
> *Barbara: Why would he worry about that?*
> *Andrew: They would capture and torture him. They weren't your "Hi, I'm your nice neighbor" type.*
> *Barbara: Are you confusing Nineveh of then with Iraq of today?*
> *Andrew: No! Even then there was conflict between Israel and Assyria.*
> *Barbara: I'm sorry. You are right. There always were armies, debates, and travel.*

Barbara relishes the moments when students open up the discussion, and she is not about to close off possibilities by answering Debby's question herself. Remembering that Andrew identified Nineveh with Iraq earlier, Barbara checks out on which historical plane he is operating. When it is clear Andrew has his history straight, she apologizes and reinforces his point. Andrew then turns the discussion from Jonah to God.

> *Andrew: Why does God care about them? They [the*
> *people of Nineveh] don't even believe in God.*
> *Barbara: That's a great question!*
> *Debby: He wanted to be the God of everyone.*
> *Barbara: You mean that His laws are for everyone.*
> *Andrew: It doesn't work that way.*
> *Staci: That's why you have a prophet.*
> *Barbara: You mean that from our perspective, as peo-*
> *ple who believe in God, we want His word to get to them,*
> *and how can it get there without a prophet?*
> *Staci: Yes.*
> *Andrew: Why should he [Jonah] go? They won't*
> *believe him. They will probably torture him.*
> *Debby: If he's scared they will capture him, he should*
> *realize God wouldn't ask him if it was going to hurt him.*
> *Barbara: He should have more faith. If it is not in his*
> *best interest, it is in the best interest of humanity.*
> *Andrew: A prophet of God wouldn't run unless he*
> *had a good reason.*

The students now enter the Jonah story with the force of their imaginations as they try to understand the actions of God and Jonah. Andrew is the pragmatist in the discussion. Why should God care about these people who do not even believe in Him? Why should Jonah undertake this mission to Nineveh if it is not likely to succeed and if he will end up being tortured for delivering the unwelcome message? Debby and Staci see God as having an important mission to accomplish through the prophet Jonah and as providing Jonah with the needed protection against the wrath of Nineveh. Andrew seems less certain about divine protection. In his view Jonah the prophet would not be fleeing unless he had good cause to do so.

Seeing the students' involvement, Barbara limits her role to amplifying their comments and drawing out more explicitly the theological assumptions of the story as she understands them. I am struck by how well these students intuit the main themes of the book. The questions of why the God of Israel should care about the people of Nineveh and what the role of the prophet is in relation to God's caring are central to Jonah, as scholars have indicated.[7]

Rebekka enters the conversation with a comment that alters the frame of reference. "Maybe Jonah didn't know. If God spoke to you, you'd think you were crazy."

Once Rebekka injects a note of modern skepticism, Barbara tries to separate the realms of now and then. "Certainly in modern times. Remember this was written a long time ago. We have records of people saying that God spoke to them, and we are not sure what they meant." Barbara wants to preserve the possibility that certain people in biblical times had a relationship with God that we do not commonly have. While not insisting upon a literal reading of the Bible, she wants to expand the possibilities beyond Rebekka's assumption that God's speaking to you is "crazy."

I had seen Barbara in past classes perform this teaching maneuver with grace. When a student crosses the lines between current and biblical realities, she reminds the students of the cultural and historical gaps as a way of preserving the integrity of both eras. But this time Barbara follows this maneuver by asking, "What would we say today that might be like God's speaking to you? Did you ever do something that you feel fits in with what God says?"

No student responds. There is a moment of awkward silence. Instead of returning the discussion back to Jonah, she has followed Rebekka's lead and asks about people's current relationship to God. That is a conversation-stopper.

Barbara breaks the silence by suggesting that in doing *tzedakah* (acts of justice), "sometimes people feel they are doing what God says." Rebekka responds by admitting that possibility, but adds, "I've never felt that way."

Remaining in the present, Barbara asks: "Did you ever feel close to God?"

> *Rebekka: I've never had a conversation with God.*
> *Nancy: I feel closer at temple, at a service.*
> *Barbara: Sometimes when I hear music I feel closer to God.*

> *Nancy: Why?*
>
> *Barbara: I feel a connection to something much bigger than myself. I know that music is composed and played by people, but what it does to my feelings is more than a people feeling. Sometimes when I climb a mountain I also have that feeling. Don't you ever feel that way?*
>
> *Debby: I have a good feeling from that, but it is like a good accomplishment.*
>
> *Staci: Not God. I don't believe in God. It is something else, but not God.*

Barbara takes the risk of sharing her own religious experience with the students, but they mostly do not connect. Outside the frame of studying Jonah, they return to a familiar secular discourse in which climbing a mountain leaves one feeling accomplished, not closer to God. When asked if she ever feels close to God, Rebekka translates the question into the rather concrete category of having "a conversation with God" and misses the more subtle connection that Barbara is suggesting. Finally Staci's comment, "Not God. I don't believe in God," is a firm signal to Barbara that the God discussion can proceed no further. Barbara heeds Staci's signal, quickly brings the discussion to a close, and brings the focus back to answering questions in Hebrew about Jonah.

An hour-and-a-half class changes the dynamics of the interaction. Barbara does not have to worry about being caught by the bell in mid-sentence, but she does have to be sensitive to time rhythms and to the students' need to take a break from the intensity of a single curricular focus. She concludes the discussion at around 4:55 and the lesson on Jonah at 5:00, one hour into the class. That is the usual time for a break; but what is unusual today is that the discussion ends abruptly and without resolution. Barbara usually ends such discussions with a summative statement reviewing the topic under consideration. Today she simply notes Staci's comment and shifts gears from conversation in English to questions in Hebrew. The question is, why did she make the abrupt shift?

Reviewing the transcript closely revealed two significant foci or frames to this discussion. The first was established by Debby when she commented, "I don't understand why Jonah did not want to do what God asked." This frame—the relationship between God and Jonah—was sustained by the group for some time because the students had much to say about that relationship. Within the frame of studying the biblical story, no one—including Staci—had any problem relating to God as a character in the story.

As noted previously, Rebekka was the first to change that focus by commenting that "If God spoke to you, you'd think you were crazy." She did this not to disrupt the discussion, but to join it. As seen with the eighth-graders, it is not unusual for the students to move rapidly between the God of the Bible and the God of today. In that move, however, they almost inevitably inject, as Rebekka did, a note of modern skepticism. It is as if they cannot fully sustain the discussion of the text without reminding the group that on the issue of God they are skeptics.

Barbara's usual tack is to restore the original frame by separating the Bible from current times. Thus her move to stay with the second frame and address head-on the God of the present was surprising. And here Heilman is helpful; for as he notes, once the teacher represents a traditional position that differs substantially from the modern worldview of the students, the students experience the tension of the dissonance. They find it difficult to sustain the discussion and may "flood out"—that is, they may find ways to move "out of play." That involves either stopping to pay attention or acting out in disruptive ways.[8]

These students experience the dissonance—the inability to connect to what Barbara is offering—but they do not flood out. They listen as she talks of feeling close to God, and Nancy even joins the conversation. But once Barbara asks, "Don't you ever feel that way?" they back off until Staci directly states that God is not part of her life. Barbara is skilled enough as a teacher to hear their message and breaks the frame herself by closing the discussion and changing the subject. She instantaneously knows that she has taken the issue of God as far as the students can handle it. To persist would be to risk their flooding out. Even summarizing must feel precarious, since at that point the students are no longer in this discussion.

It takes courage for Barbara to put herself on the line and risk the students' seeing her beliefs as different or strange. Had she stayed within the bounds of the Jonah story, the discussion probably would have ended on a high note. Why then did Barbara switch frames, and what do we learn from what resulted?

A year earlier I observed Barbara teaching this same chapter of Jonah to the preceding seventh grade. The question arose in class of why God, who is thought of as being omnipotent, so clearly needs Jonah to deliver His message to Nineveh. Why not deliver the message by Himself and forget about the reluctant Jonah?

The class struggled with whether the God of the Bible is omnipotent and why God seems to need human beings. At the end of an engaging and thoughtful discussion that did not yield clear answers, Barbara concluded: "We have a story that does not provide a lot of answers; but it raises a lot of good questions so that we can think about these issues in a Jewish way."

Barbara has little interest in providing answers but much interest in raising questions that stretch the students' thinking and challenge their assumptions. Although in the other classes I observed she limited those questions to the text, she is the kind of teacher who shares herself with her students. She identifies herself as a Reform Jew and wants to share that Judaism with them. In this class she chooses to share her experiences of closeness to God. Even though that experience does not emanate directly from the text, she is suggesting a link between what the prophet experienced of God and what we today can experience. It is that link that the students cannot follow or even tolerate.

There is an irony in comparing this class to that of Rachel's eighth-grade class. Although Rachel, in a style more characteristic of this school, keeps the conversation as best she could directed at the God of Exodus and keeps her own beliefs out of the discussion, she manages to sustain the frame of examining Exodus only until the bell rings. Then the students break that frame to declare their contemporary skepticism. Barbara more directly confronts the students by herself switching frames, while her students, with perhaps the exception of Rebekka, would have remained comfortably within the biblical frame. But in both classes the students have the final say. The moral and epistemological assumptions that inform their secular worldview rule out for the moment a belief in God in any form that they can comprehend. That is not true for all the students, but it is for most who expressed themselves.

The conversation between teacher and students will continue. The students in both classes will return in the following weeks to continue studying Bible and expressing their distance from God and Judaism. They may withhold their recognition of God, but through their continued study, they remain in some relationship with the God they deny. To put it differently, they remain in a relationship with teachers like Barbara and Rachel who continue to represent a perspective on Jewish tradition that they as modern adolescents cannot fully affirm.

The dance that Barbara and her students perform in this class—in which she reveals as much of her own Jewish beliefs as she chooses before retreating before their growing discomfort—is not a limited, one-time event. In a sense, whenever a teacher at Temple Akiba represents a traditional perspective that is foreign to modern sensibilities, she risks placing distance between herself and her students and crossing the line of their tolerance for cultural and religious dissonance. To cross the line could lead to the students' flooding out or withdrawing; but to not approach the line is to give up on teaching the Judaism that this synagogue and school represent. Thus the better teachers are often involved in the dance, expressing their own identities as Jews while allowing their students to discover the aspects of that identity that at their age they can and cannot affirm.

With Our Identities on the Line

In Rachel and Barbara's classes, teachers and students

handled the dissonance between their own worldviews and that of the traditional text. But in those classes the clash between tradition and modernity remains the subtext to the actual study of the biblical text. An observation of Norman Davidman's high school class on Reform Judaism will show what happens when the clash between tradition and modernity become the explicit theme of the lesson itself.

Throughout the religious school little formal emphasis is placed on teaching Reform Judaism. It is Judaism that is being taught and *Reform* is the adjective used to explain differences in practices and beliefs from traditional or Orthodox Judaism. The first formal teaching of Reform Judaism comes in a seven-week course, co-taught by Norman Davidman and Sam Pearlman and offered to eighth- and ninth-graders. This particular class in November is taught by Norman Davidman to a combined group of twenty-five students, for Sam is out sick. This is a second-hour high school class, running from 7:30 to 8:30 P.M.

The topic of the class is the immigration of German Jews to the United States in the mid-nineteenth century and their founding of the Reform movement in this country. Norman's style of teaching is to direct questions at the students as a way of advancing the learning. He tends to be more directive than either Rachel or Barbara.

The week before the students had traced back their own family backgrounds to the countries from which their grandparents or great grandparents had emigrated. A large map of the world is posted at the front of the class and is covered with pins to designate lands of origin. There is a real diversity of locations. Although the largest cluster of pins are in the lands of Central and Eastern Europe, there are also pins in Ireland, Greece, Turkey, Egypt, Iraq, Venezuela and China. Some pins are located within the United States to indicate an earlier period of settlement in this country.

Norman Davidman distributes blank maps of the United States and asks the class to mark where the Jews from Germany settled in this country.

> *Amy: In the West, along the Pacific coast.*
> *Jeremy: In the East.*
> *Peter: In New York.*
> *Norman: Did your grandparents all come from this city?*
> *Voices: No!*
> *Norman: Drawing on your own family patterns, where did the German Jews go?*
> *Sara: Ellis Island, New York.*
> *Norman: I see your problem. This is true for your grandparents and great grandparents, but not for the German Jews who followed other Germans up the rivers of this country and settled primarily in the inland cities, such as Pittsburgh and Cincinnati.*

Drawing on their own family experience does not lead the students to the answers that work for this lesson. They offer answers typical of the immigration of Eastern European Jews in the late nineteenth and early twentieth century. Yet what goes unmentioned are the histories of those families whose stories fit the pattern of neither German or Eastern European immigration. Those stories will not be explicitly represented in this lesson on Reform Judaism.

Tying this history of German Jews to the origins of Temple Akiba, Norman tells of a discovery he made.

> When Rabbi Marcus and I came to Temple Akiba, the temple was celebrating an important anniversary, and we put together a prayer book that took examples from the congregation's history. The first prayer book used here was in Hebrew and German. These people were very comfortable in German.

The students do not appear to be moved by this story. Nor are they connecting to the origins of Reform Judaism. Perhaps sensing this, Norman moves on to the more controversial aspects of this history; the reforms that the rabbis of this movement introduced in Jewish ritual practice.

He focuses on a particular change, the rabbinic decision to stop wearing a head covering while leading the worship service. He asks the students to imagine a scene more than a hundred years earlier when on the eve of Yom Kippur, the holiest night of the liturgical calendar, the Jews are assembled in their American congregation and for the first time see that their rabbi is officiating with his head uncovered. This is a serious break with the tradition of covering one's head in prayer, especially when leading a synagogue service. The congregants are in shock. Some protest and disrupt the service. It is a jarring experience for them.

Switching to the present, Norman asks, "That is not shocking to anyone here, is it?" Having constructed this narrative to help the students understand the nineteenth-century Jews' sense of shock at seeing a bareheaded rabbi, Norman assumes the students realize this is no longer shocking, that this quickly became the norm in Reform congregations and that he and the other clergy at Temple Akiba almost always officiate without a head covering. Yet Julian seems to have missed that point. "Rabbis usually wear them." Norman asks, "Here?" and Julian responds, "Yes." Norman responds, "No, not here."

Norman then asks the class, "What is this matter of covering your head?"

> *Jacob: You're supposed to.*
> *Norman: Why?*
> *Jacob: It's in the Torah.*
> *Norman: In the Torah?*
> *Jeremy: In the Ten Commandments.*
> *Norman: You can find that in the Ten Commandments?*
> *Laura: It's a matter of respect.*
> *Reuben: It's what the Orthodox do.*
> *Norman: Based on?*
> *Reuben: Tradition.*

The traditional head cover, called kippah in Hebrew and yarmulkah in Yiddish, does not appear in Jewish literature until the Talmud and does not gain the force of law until medieval times. Jews may have begun the practice earlier, but there is certainly no evidence of its common practice in biblical literature.[9] Yet the students seem unaware of this history, and their answers are diffuse and confused. Norman seems annoyed that Jeremy would think that this custom originates in one of the Ten Commandments, but he is willing to settle for "tradition" as the basis of wearing a kippah. He summarizes by saying, "It is a matter of respect, and tradition obligates all men at all times to cover their heads."

If tradition so obligates men, then why, Norman asks, did these nineteenth-century Reform rabbis "decide to depart from this well-established norm?"

> *Jeff: To make a point.*
> *Norman: What point?*
> *Iris: If you are not happy with it, change it.*
> *Norman: They were rebels?*
> *Rena: They saw the changes and decided to change with the times.*
> *Sharon: It is possible to be a good Jew without doing all the stupid little things.*
> *Norman: Why "stupid"?*
> *Sharon: OK, traditional.*
> *Norman: Yes, unnecessary for that time.*

The students come alive in answering why people change an established traditional practice. Several hands shoot into the air at once and the tentativeness of the earlier responses gives way to more self-assured views. The students seem to identify with the modernizing impulse of the nineteenth-century rabbis.

The most telling interchange is between Sharon and Norman. Sharon gets the spirit of the early reformers right in implying a difference between the essentials of being "a good Jew" and all the "little things" that tradition demands. But in calling them "stupid little things," Sharon draws Norman's objection: "Why 'stupid?' " He wants the students to understand the reforming impulse that so strongly influenced the early history of this movement, but not to identify as stupid the concrete traditions that the reformers put aside. When Amy, following Sharon, draws an analogy between these Jewish reformers and the earlier Christian humanists who wished to distinguish biblical religion from the later increments of tradition, Norman responds, "Very good." Traditions like head covering were not stupid, but were viewed as not essential for an authentically modern Judaism.

Moving back to the nineteenth century, Norman asks, "How in those days did the majority pray?" Getting no response, he adds, "Who were the majority?" Several students respond "the Christians," and there is some nervous laughter accompanying that response.

> *Norman: What was the majority form of worship?*
> *Bill: Judaism.*
> *Norman: I can't believe you.*
> *Ted: Protestant.*
> *Norman: How do Protestants pray?*
> *Alison: We don't know; we're Jewish.*

Alison's response is followed by an outbreak of noise from all around the room. Suddenly everyone is talking at once. The lesson is now touching a nerve among the students; they are plainly anxious, and Alison is articulating their anxiety. I believe she is saying, "Rabbi, why are you asking us how Protestants pray? Don't you realize we are Jewish and wouldn't know that?" Yet one student takes the risk of responding.

> *Jill: I went to a Christian service.*
> *Norman: Good. What did they wear on their heads?*
> *Jill: Nothing. Well, maybe the big guy wore something.*
> *Amy: The big guy?*

Jill's rough reference to the minister or priest as "the big guy" sends a current through the room, and again everyone is talking at once. Norman has to stop the lesson to let them know he is waiting to continue. When they have quieted down, he continues the lesson, probably aware that time is now running out. "If the majority culture prays without the head covered, what does it mean when a rabbi does that on Yom Kippur?"

> *Craig: That he's crazy.*
> *Emily: Rebellion.*
> *Scott: The opposite of rebellion. It's conformity.*
> *Norman: Listen!*
> *Scott: The Jews were the rebels. He is conforming to other people's religion.*

Norman likes Scott's response and elaborates upon it in his final, summarizing remark.

> It was an act of assimilating. But there were many reasons for doing it: to keep up with the times, to get rid of what was unnecessary *in their eyes*—like the Christian humanists. Finally, it was an act of rebellion *and* conformity. You look less obviously Jewish if your head is uncovered. I cannot separate out the reasons.

By now it is 8:30 P.M., and the class is over. The students exit quickly and leave Norman and me alone to talk for a minute. I am fascinated by how he constructed his narrative about the head covering and ended the lesson without taking sides over whether this was an act of rebellion or conformity. I say, "In the end you neither defend nor put down the reformer's practice, but give both sides of the argument." Norman simply responds, "That's right. It's a complex issue."

This class ends on a very different note from that of the classes I observed Norman teach in Bible. In those classes, he seems quite certain of the positions he takes. To be sure, he may leave the students with questions to consider, but he seems to feel in complete control of the material. In this class *he* seems to feel more tentative, more genuinely open to the two sides of the argument.

A subsequent conversation with Rachel Abeles helped me to better understand what I observed here. In her view Norman is divided in his own evaluation of the early days of the Reform movement. He admires the courage of these early reformers to innovate, to seize the spirit of their times and to break openly with those aspects of Jewish tradition that no longer spoke to them. Yet, their innovation, as this example illustrates, often involved a rejection of tradition, a stripping away of the bark of unessential tradition from the tree of "authentic Judaism." In his rabbinical role, Norman has largely moved in the other direction by often choosing to restore the traditions that his predecessors removed. While he admires their courage, he rejects their identifying *progress* and *reform* with the tendency to assimilate into the majority culture. He is uneasy when Jews adopt the worship practices of Protestant churches. Yet he does not wish to be religiously obligated to any tradition, such as wearing a kippah, if that tradition does not intrinsically add to his Jewish sense of himself.

In an interview Norman reported that he grew up in a classical Reform congregation and loved it. He views classical Reform Judaism as a complex and subtle mixture of elements and not simply as an assimilationist movement. Perhaps he chooses to teach this course to convey to the next generation some of this complex evaluation of the past.

But what can the eighth- and ninth-graders make of this subtle acceptance and rejection of the early Reform movement? As Rachel suggested when we discussed this class, the students seem barely aware of the major distinctions at play here. She doubts that the students make any clear distinctions between Judaism and Reform Judaism. They know they are Jews, but are not Orthodox. That makes them Reform, which is hard to distinguish from Conservative. They are not aware of the historical distinction between German and Eastern European Jews and certainly not of the differences between classical and contemporary Reform Judaism. If they realize that Temple Akiba dates back to the nineteenth century, they do not seem very interested in learning about its German-speaking founders.

Yet somewhere along the way this lesson clearly grabs their attention. The class begins with the students unfocused and the teacher doing most of the talking. But once Norman begins telling the story of the rabbi with the uncovered head, almost all twenty-five students become involved. Can the story be that powerful?

Norman told the story dramatically and played up the opposition of some members of the congregation to this break from tradition. The students seemed drawn in by the double drama: that of the story itself and that of their senior rabbi narrating a tale about a rabbi who shocked his congregation with his untraditional behavior. That interplay—authority figure telling in positive tones of a rebellion against authority—captured the attention of this adolescent audience.

The class discussion peaked in intensity when Norman asked the class to consider why the rabbi would have departed from this well-established norm. The students almost entirely identify with the rabbi's impulse to change with the times and have ready answers to share as to why tradition should make way for modernity.

But the discussion suddenly goes off track when Norman asks them how the majority culture worshiped at that time. The rabbi's asking them to talk about Christian worship leaves the students uncomfortable. At first they hesitate to identify the majority as Christian; then they laugh nervously at the identification. When Norman asks, "How do Protestants pray?" he seems to be requesting straightforward information; but they seem to hear the question as a personal one. When Alison retorts, "We don't know; we're Jewish," everyone starts talking in all corners of the room.

This anxious outburst is what Heilman calls "flooding out." The tension that was initiated by Norman's question and signaled by the nervous laughter comes to a crescendo with the probe about Protestant worship. Alison's response occasions the release of the tension and the thunderstorm of comments from across the room. The question to consider is what is the source of this incredible tension.

On many levels this history lesson has become a conversation about identity, or, what Barbara Myerhoff calls an occasion "to develop their collective identity." Perhaps it is to be expected that a course on Reform Judaism will become self-referential and deal with the Jewish identity of the members of the class. Yet there are two conversations going on at once. One is about the relation of tradition to modernity and the other about the relation of Jews to the Christian majority culture. The former was the announced topic; the latter seemed to have surfaced without advanced warning.

The students, while not well-informed about who wears a kippah and why, use the controversy to express strong views on tradition and modernity. As in the other classes we observed, students voice both sides of the issue. The majority tend to value the claims of modernity more and worry less about the diminution of tradition. Only Scott defends Jewish tradition and views the rabbi's adapting to modernity as conformity to the majority culture. Even at 8:30 P.M., the students clearly enjoy engaging in this debate.

But the other identity issue that surfaces in this class—the one that Don Marcus spoke about in the teacher orientation: what does it mean to be a Jew in a non-Jewish society?—is less comfortable for the students to discuss. It enters the discussion through a side door and causes as great anxiety as it did for the teachers at orientation. What is the source of the anxiety?

Heilman teaches us to look for the source of the anxiety in the dissonance between the material and perspective represented by the teacher and the worldview of the students. But in this class, as opposed to Barbara's class on Jonah, Norman is not introducing a dissonant view of God, but asking a question about American culture. Why should that question be experienced as so dissonant?

A careful review of the transcript reveals that the students may have been caught off guard by a switch in frames. They had been discussing with Norman the basis in Jewish tradition for wearing a kippah and the motivations of the rabbi for breaking with that tradition. As those questions seemed to be answered, he then switched to the questions about majority culture. While Norman knew where the questions were leading, the students might have felt at a loss.

The sudden switch can perhaps explain the students' awkwardness in answering the initial questions. But Alison's response—"We don't know; we're Jewish"—indicates that more is going on than frame confusion. Why does Alison have to mention to the rabbi that "we're Jewish?" Is it not evident by their being there that they are Jewish?

I suggest that Alison's comment operates in much the same way as Staci's comment did in Barbara's class. Staci's "Not God. I don't believe in God" signals to Barbara to proceed no further with the discussion of closeness to God. Alison makes her comment to signal to Norman that his questions have become too threatening, that his assumption that they would know about church practice is causing them much anxiety. If he recognizes them as Jews, why is he, the rabbi, asking them these questions?

Keeping in mind the nature of the learning in this class and what Don told the teachers at orientation, we can make sense of the anxiety. When the students become engaged by the narrative Norman constructed, they enter the class discussion with that wonderful adolescent sense of freshness and excitement. In the discussion these students find the opportunity to perform who they are as Jews. They await the opportunity with anticipation, but also with a sense of vulnerability. What if the identity that one articulates proves unacceptable to the partners in the discussion? What if the rabbi—that eminent figure of Jewish authority—finds your Jewishness lacking?

The height of vulnerability for these students lies, as Don suggested to his teachers, in the possibility that one's very identity as a Jew will be called into question by the family links one has to Christianity. This lesson began with reference to that map of the world and all the pins that indicate the lands of origin of one's predecessors. While never spoken about, the location of the pins reflect clearly enough that some of these children come from non-Jewish families who did not come over with either the Jews of Germany or Eastern Europe. They know that, and the rabbi knows that. They are vulnerable.

"We don't know; we're Jewish" is Alison's way of protecting the class from their collective vulnerability. If Norman is implying that they have knowledge about Christian practice that could call their status as Jews into question, he needs to be warned that he is crossing onto their vulnerable ground. As in Barbara's class, there comes a point when the students feel threatened and then signal to the teacher "this far and no further."

As in a social drama described by Turner, this is a crisis moment. At such liminal moments the discussion can either fall apart or find alternative routes. In this case Jill provided the alternative route, and in almost no time, the frame had switched back to the more comfortable conversation about tradition and modernity. The danger of flooding out receded, and Norman could bring the lesson to its anticipated conclusion.

Here we witness a different "dance" from the one in Barbara's class. Barbara chose to push her students' tolerance by introducing her thoughts on closeness to God. She then read their signals and aborted the conversation before reaching the point of flooding out. Norman, without conscious intent, suddenly switched frames and very quickly crossed a line, which engendered their flooding out. But by holding steady and waiting for assistance from a student, he managed to contain the damage and salvage the discussion.

What is again evident is how dynamic the interaction is once these adolescents become engaged. There is no simple learning process going on. Rather, there is a very complex social drama unfolding. The students, by opening themselves up to the questions raised by the material, seize the opportunity to enact their identities as Jews, but they also guard very carefully their vulnerabilities. They swiftly erect lines of defense that the teacher needs to respect and treat with care.

To teach well in these classes one needs to elicit serious interest, be genuine in presenting one's Judaism, and yet be sensitive to the dissonance created. Above all, as Don warned his teachers on the first day, one has to be aware of how vulnerable are the Jewish identities of some of these students. Their Jewishness is not a given. It needs to be demonstrated, examined, and defended with each clash between tradition and modernity.

Rabbi Marcus' opening remarks at the orientation ring true throughout our observations. Children and youth need a lot of reassurance that they belong. The impressive educational structure that this synagogue has built rests on the faith assumption that a few hours a week of quality Jewish education will touch the hearts of children who come from such diverse Jewish backgrounds. Don Marcus never forgets the essential point: teach as impressively as possible, but it is the human relationships that will keep these youth coming back. Build those relationships, and with all their doubts and confusions, youth will return for further dialogue and debate.

Chapter 5
The "Mandatory Hebrew" Controversy

At this point we turn to examine the place of the school within the synagogue community; for little of significance takes places within the school that is not influenced by larger trends within the life of the congregation.

The focus of this chapter is on the "mandatory Hebrew" controversy that erupted in the middle of the school year at Temple Akiba. This controversy had its origins in a decision made by the Religious School Committee (RSC), a lay body charged with the responsibility for setting educational policy for the religious school. Working closely with Rabbi Marcus, this committee decided after much deliberation to make the learning of Hebrew a mandatory requirement for all the students in the religious school. When their decision ran into fierce, unforeseen parental opposition, these lay leaders had to decide how to respond to the opposition. The decisions they made in consultation with Rabbi Marcus—as well as the process they used to arrive at them—are the focus of this chapter.

The "mandatory Hebrew" controversy followed by one month the family education program described in Chapter 2. Viewed in retrospect, the two appear to have a strong connection. Both may be described as social dramas, and both illustrate the importance of social drama within the life of the congregation. But the "mandatory Hebrew" controversy was larger in scope, since it involved Rabbi Marcus, the members of the RSC, the protesting parents, and, peripherally, the board of the synagogue. In full it extended over a period of several months. Yet, it may be surprising to see how much overlap there is between these two dramas.

Following Turner's framework, the "mandatory Hebrew" controversy was a clash in normative values that set two groups within the same organization on a collision course with one another. The RSC, guided by one set of values, put forward a policy change that ran directly against the views of members who perceived the change as threatening to their own value positions within the congregation. The resulting collision lasted only briefly, but it afforded me the opportunity to see more clearly the resistance to the policies that have been championed by Rabbis Davidman and Marcus. It also made visible how the lay leaders who most closely support the rabbis' vision of education handled the opposition of a minority who do not completely share that vision. Studying this social drama will illuminate how ongoing conflicts within the culture of the synagogue come to crisis in the educational domain and require careful handling if the educational agenda is to move forward without causing a split in the membership.

In the previous chapters I have made the claim that Temple Akiba has been committed to providing quality Jewish education to both its children and adult members. I have tried to illustrate how the rabbis and educators have been translating that commitment into educational programs for adults, families, and children. Yet, I have not hidden the difficulties and conflicts involved, but have stressed the impressive educational achievements observable at this synagogue.

Here I will deal more directly with the resistance to the changes proposed by the rabbis and supported by key lay leaders. On numerous occasions, some reported in earlier chapters, I heard congregants, often parents of school-age children, call into question one or another aspect of the rabbis' educational vision. None of these undermine the congregation's basic commitment to providing quality Jewish education. Rather, they express the unease that some feel over the implications of curricular change for the life of Temple Akiba. It is less the curricular changes themselves that arouse the opposition than the values embedded in those changes as perceived by some of the members. It is not simply a case of resistance to change, but a questioning of which change should take precedence in a synagogue culture that is constantly undergoing multiple changes.

This detailed account of the "mandatory Hebrew" controversy illustrates that even in a congregation with a strong commitment to providing quality Jewish education, there is no easy or unchallenged route to gaining consensus. By tracing that lack of consensus to value conflicts within the culture of the congregation, I hope to show that educational decision-making must be viewed on the wider screen that is the history and culture of the congregation.[1]

Hebrew at Temple Akiba

Since the early decades of this century, Temple Akiba has prided itself in providing quality Reform Jewish education. But until the 1940s the religious school met once a week and did not include the teaching of Hebrew as a major part of the curriculum. Since religious services in those years were conducted primarily in English and as classical Reform Judaism was non-Zionist in orientation, there was little perceived need for teaching Hebrew to either children or adults.

With a transition in rabbinic leadership in the 1940s came two significant changes in temple philosophy that affected the place of Hebrew in the temple. First, more traditional prayers and rituals (including Bar Mitzvah) were introduced into the liturgy. Second, the leadership became more supportive of the Zionist cause of establishing a Jewish homeland and reviving Hebrew as a spoken language. After World War II, the temple opened a regular Hebrew program for students in the school for the first time.

This new Hebrew program, described in Chapter 3, was neither mandatory nor fully integrated into the existing religious school. Religious school continued to meet on Sunday. Those students who wished to learn Hebrew came during the week to the voluntary Hebrew program. The religious school education culminated in the confirmation ceremony, which was held after tenth grade. The Hebrew education culminated in Bar Mitzvah at age thirteen.

Over the years, as more and more families wanted their children to become Bar or Bat Mitzvah, the midweek Hebrew program grew in popularity, for to become Bar or Bat Mitzvah a child has to know enough Hebrew to participate in the Hebraized Shabbat service.

When Rabbi Davidman came to Temple Akiba, he expressed a serious interest in making Jewish and particularly Hebrew education central to the mission of the synagogue. Since becoming the temple educator, Rabbi Marcus has been working to implement serious curricular reform in the way that Hebrew and Bible are taught. He chose to use the Melton Hebrew Language Program, which places the learning of classical Hebrew at the forefront of the curricular agenda. Recognizing that students in a part-time program cannot be expected to learn both modern and classical Hebrew, the rabbis agreed with the designers of the Melton curriculum that priority should be given to learning to read and comprehend the classical Hebrew texts that constitute much of Jewish ritual life. Learning modern Hebrew could be left for the higher grades once the students had mastered the elements of classical Hebrew.[2]

This decision was unusual for several reasons. First, the Melton curriculum was developed for use in the Conservative movement, and this is a Reform synagogue school. Second, even most Conservative schools have not adopted this Melton curriculum, since its prioritizing of classical Hebrew is not commonly accepted in the field. Third, adopting this curriculum requires retraining the teachers to learn its philosophy and methods. Retraining has not commonly been done in synagogue schools since few synagogues will invest serious time and money in training teachers who work part-time and who may leave after a couple of years.

At Temple Akiba the denominational issue was not a factor. The faculty has used a wide variety of curricula and text materials without much attention paid to denominational origin. But retraining of teachers was a factor. Don Marcus realized early on that without the temple's committing itself to assembling and training a competent staff of Hebrew teachers, there would be no chance that this curricular reform could yield positive results. The steps he took to build this staff have been documented in Chapter 3.

Of the ten teachers teaching in the five grades of the Hebrew program, I observed eight of them and found a wide range in their teaching skill, from the veterans who were outstanding to one new teacher who could barely manage his class. In the middle were the majority, who clearly knew how to manage their classes, organize their lessons, and relate to their students, but were still learning to master the curriculum. They were regularly supervised by the Hebrew coordinator.

The class studying Jonah (described in Chapter 4), which was taught by a veteran in the Hebrew program, showed that students who have pursued the program seriously from grades three to seven emerge able to read a biblical text in the original and, with the help of a dictionary, to translate and read with comprehension. They ask meaningful questions of the text and, in guided discussions, engage in a process of inquiry regarding the meaning of the biblical narrative. They also have a rudimentary capacity to speak simple sentences in modern Hebrew. Those students who have not pursued their studies as consistently show a capacity to read fluently but are less able to comprehend and translate the text. They are unlikely to be able to speak modern Hebrew.

As an observer, I have suggested that Temple Akiba has much to be proud of in this Hebrew program.[3] The majority of students in the Hebrew program take it seriously, attend regularly, pay attention in class, do homework, and show incremental gains in the mastery of Hebrew. The teachers and parents with whom I spoke are quite satisfied with the program and feel that serious learning is taking place. A vast majority of the students attending three days a week continue their Jewish education beyond Bar or Bat Mitzvah in the Temple Akiba high school.

Should Hebrew Be Mandatory?

The policy for the Hebrew program remained that attendance at this midweek Hebrew program was optional for students. There were only twenty-five students in the religious school who chose the non-Hebrew option. These students came for the three hours on Sunday and took as one of their courses Synagogue Skills, whose aim was to prepare them to participate in the temple's religious services. This involved learning to read Hebrew. From my observations, the sixth-grade students' capacity to decode remained quite limited and stood in stark contrast to that of their peers in the Hebrew program.

In the spring of 1989, Rabbi Marcus proposed to the RSC that the time had come to consider whether "to make Hebrew mandatory."[4] If adopted by the RSC, which is responsible for setting the Hebrew policy for the school, and approved by the synagogue's board of trustees, this proposal would have the practical effect of eliminating the option of students attending religious school for only one day a week. It would require that every student from third to seventh grade study Hebrew in a midweek program. Students would have the choice of attending the three-days-a-week Hebrew program or attending school on Sunday and arranging a Hebrew tutorial at home during the week. The tutorial arrangement was discouraged by the school, but chosen at extra cost by a sizable minority of families.

This proposal also had symbolic implications for Temple Akiba. It would mean the synagogue's affirming the importance of learning Hebrew in the Jewish education of all the children, and, by implication, affirming that knowing Hebrew is an important element in being a knowledgeable Jew. This change in policy would symbolically reverse the vision of an earlier period of classical Reform Judaism when Hebrew played a minor role in the temple's religious life and study programs were conducted almost entirely in English.

Don Marcus had a close relationship with the members of the current RSC. He had been working to develop a more informed and consistent lay leadership who could advise him on matters of educational policy. The question of whether to make Hebrew mandatory grew out of the work they had been doing together in reviewing and evaluating the religious school curriculum. They had come to realize that learning Hebrew was a vital part of the school's curriculum.[5] They wondered why there was still the option available to receive a religious education at Temple Akiba without learning Hebrew beyond the most minimal level.

Although Don favored this proposal, he did not press for its immediate approval, for in its first deliberations the committee was quite divided over the wisdom of making Hebrew mandatory and eliminating the Sunday-only option. Those opposed had two reservations. Given the history of this temple, making Hebrew mandatory would be seen as a reversal of the once-dominant classical Reform ideology that still had adherents in the congregation. Additionally, eliminating the Sunday-only option might result in squeezing out certain groups of families who clustered around that option.

The result of the RSC's first vote was so close that Don suggested they postpone a decision until there was time to study carefully the questions that had been raised. He was particularly concerned about whether the effect of this change would be to exclude the "marginal" families. Having worked hard to open Temple Akiba to more interfaith, single-parent, and New American families, he did not want to undo that work by unintentionally pushing them out of the religious school.

A careful review of the data on which families had chosen the Sunday-only option revealed that no single type of family was over-represented in that population. Learning that, Don and Sherry Saunders, the committee chairperson, went back to the RSC a year later to ask for a second consideration of the issue. After deliberating again, the RSC voted by a wider majority to approve making Hebrew mandatory for all students in the religious school. They concluded, in the words of their chairperson, that "the study of Hebrew is the linchpin of making possible a richer understanding of the history, liturgy, and literature of the Jewish people." Therefore, "allowing even a small percentage of our population not to study Hebrew was inconsistent with our philosophy and goals." While "fully aware of the discomfort" this would cause some families, the committee based their decision on the "long-standing tradition of excellence in our religious school education."[6]

I was invited to be an observer of the RSC's process after this decision had been made. At its December meeting, the first that I attended, the RSC was considering how to present this change in policy to the parent body of the religious school. In addition to notifying the parents in writing that this change would go into effect for the next school year, the committee decided to call an open meeting in January for parents and interested temple members to discuss the change as well as other issues on the committee's agenda. The committee sensed there would be some concern but did not fully anticipate what would occur. The open meeting became a forum for very heated disagreement by dissenting parents who felt this change was a total reversal of longstanding temple policy of offering members a choice of how they wished to educate their children and, indeed, how they wished to define themselves as Jews.

The Open Meeting

Soon after Sherry Saunders, chair of the RSC, begins this part of the open meeting by announcing the change in policy to make Hebrew mandatory in the school, she encounters resistance. Two of the fathers want to know why, if the committee had made this decision earlier, they were being notified only in January after they had already paid their synagogue membership dues. "I might have to leave the temple and I could have made other plans," announced one father in an annoyed voice.

> *Sherry: Why are people thinking of leaving?*
> *Father 1: My kids can't go for two days, and paying an extra $950 [for tutoring] is too much.*
> *Father 2: Those of us who as kids were given*

Orthodox gobbledygook were turned off. Now this is arbitrary gobbledygook again. You don't need to know Hebrew to be Jewish!

One day a week is all the Jewish education these fathers want for their children. The second father, a survivor of an unhappy Orthodox education, identified the RSC's decision with "Orthodox gobbledygook." He could not fathom that Reform Jews would consider Hebrew essential to Jewish education. He joined this temple so his child could escape the Hebrew lessons he dreaded as a child.

Before Sherry can respond, Janet (some people at the meeting were identified by name), a mother of three older children, delivers two stinging critiques of the committee's decision.

> I am a member of the school committee [in a local town]. You are not following a process. Closed meetings are wrong. I joined this temple because it offered choice. You're removing a choice that I thought Temple Akiba stood for: a place to belong if you did it this way or that. . . . To change the rules for us is wrong. To discuss it behind closed doors is not a process. You didn't survey us.

Therefore, she implies, their decision is not valid. Janet continues:

> My husband is not Jewish and not a member of the temple. When we were deciding on which temple to join, we went from educator to educator. The educator at Temple Akiba said, "We educate kids so they will know the right questions to ask, and hopefully they will choose Reform Judaism." My husband, who is a lapsed Catholic, felt comfortable with the response. To ask the family to do more than they can support is wrong. This is Temple Akiba, where your family values will be respected. To change the rules midstream is wrong.

At stake here, in Janet's view, is not solely the question of Hebrew, but the right of a family to have their values respected. It is wrong to ask families to send their children for two or three days a week if that represents "more than they can support." Worse, it is a violation of the principle of choice which Temple Akiba stands for.

Listening to Janet, I did not think it was incidental that she began by referring to her husband who "is not Jewish." Janet knows, as does most everyone at this meeting, that in a sizable minority of the families in this school, one parent is not Jewish. The temple and the school have decided to welcome interfaith families and to respect their values as long as they are raising their children as Jews. She contended that this decision about Hebrew would be viewed as pulling back from the commitment to respect these families' values.

Janet is not alone in this concern, as another mother makes clear:

> We chose the Hebrew tutorial for our child because we could afford it. My husband is a lapsed Catholic and for him "mandatory" is a problem. I know that Bar Mitzvah is not mandatory in Reform. I'm not displeased with the Hebrew tutorial, but I don't think my family can do a Bar Mitzvah. . . . It's going to be more uncomfortable as a congregation for interfaith couples. There are a lot of interfaith couples here. . . . I'm worried about the atmosphere.

This mother did not come to complain about her child's Hebrew education. No parent at the meeting did. Rather, her concern is with "atmosphere," the delicate question of whether interfaith couples will continue to feel comfortable. She feels this curricular change will signal that they are less welcome. Although no one has proposed making Bar or Bat Mitzvah celebration mandatory, she feels that her family's decision not to celebrate a Bar Mitzvah might be viewed more negatively once Hebrew becomes mandatory.

But it is not only the intermarried members or the

refugees from Orthodoxy who are uncomfortable with this move. Three parents from other perspectives express their concerns:

> *Nancy: I grew up in this temple. Temple Akiba represented to me openness and caring. To close off even a small minority is wrong. To not give them exposure to Judaism is wrong. . . . I can't believe that you would close these people out. I am shocked!*
>
> *Carolyn: In my family my daughter will be the fifth generation to go to Sunday school and be confirmed. I'm furious! This is a Jewish way?*
>
> *Jeff: This is the first time this congregation has said, "You must do something." I want my son to be Bar Mitzvah, but maybe at age seven he's not ready [to make this commitment]. If this is a fait accompli, I may have to leave. I think this is a great temple. But, don't tell me! The "mandatory" is the issue.*

Nancy speaks on the brink of tears, Carolyn with fury on her tongue, and Jeff with a mixture of bewilderment and defiance. All three see this decision as deviating from their vision of what this temple stands for. Nancy believes a caring community would not willingly exclude any of its members. Carolyn insists that if Sunday school was right for her parents and grandparents, it should also be right for her daughter. Jeff speaks as one of the many who have been recently attracted to join. He never thought he would be told, "You must do something." To hear the word *mandatory* is jolting enough for him to consider leaving the temple.

The tone of these remarks is so emotional that another woman rises to suggest: "There is such an outcry! Couldn't you open the process in an open forum so you can hear us and then decide?" When Sherry assures her that the committee will meet to talk about this, there is a further outcry that their meeting was not enough: "You'll decide this in the closet!" Don suggests that the committee has heard the feedback and will get back to people, but that assurance also fails to calm the apprehensions. Then Ben, a psychologist and a member of the RSC, shares his reactions to what had been said:

> To me the comments about process are very important. A committee working together can get isolated, and we have. I for one will suggest that we reexamine the decision. My pledge is that the process will be discussed. Today the concerns expressed are emotionally vested and not rationally discussed. The process needs to be repaired. This committee, in its evolution and in relation to the school and temple, is in a period of growth and defining itself. It's an adolescent committee that is learning something about process. . . . Whether or not the decision is reversed, process is very important.

By stressing that the complaints about the committee's process are justified and will be considered, and by admitting that the committee itself is growing and learning—that it is actually "an adolescent committee"—Ben manages to speak to the feelings in the room and assure those in dissent that a member of the RSC has heard them and has taken their remarks seriously. After Ben's statement, Sherry can close this part of the meeting and go on to the next item on the agenda.

I was surprised by how quickly the storm settled and the meeting was able to focus on the next report. But everyone on the RSC realized that their decision had been hit by a flood of feelings and that they would have to meet again to assess the damages.

The RSC Reassesses Its Decision

At their next scheduled meeting in January, two weeks after the open meeting, the members of the RSC meet to reassess where they stand in regard to mandatory Hebrew. Don Marcus opens the discussion by reading three letters he has received from parents who had spoken up in dissent at the meeting. They are thoughtful, emotional elaborations on the themes of the meetings.

Ben picks up from where he had left off at the open meeting:

> We made a mistake in terms of process. . . . We lost touch with the constituency we represent. We see ourselves more as a committee relating to Don Marcus. We need to keep reminding ourselves of what are the ongoing issues for these parents. . . . In these letters there is a strong feeling among previous generations of Reform Jews that they are being attacked as Jews. They seem to need to prove that they are good Jews without Hebrew.

Three other members quickly agree with Ben that there were errors in process that need to be rectified before this policy decision should be implemented. But Sherry disagrees:

> We are a private institution and not a school board. We are not elected. Analogies to school committees do not speak to me. . . . You don't just vote with the constituency, but take a leadership role. We are charged with a responsibility to make a decision. In an open forum it's a given that you will hear from the dissatisfied. If we could poll the entire community, the vote might go with us.

Having once served on her town's school committee, Sherry has a different view from Ben's. She does not believe the RSC represents a constituency. The committee members are not elected by the parents or temple members; they are appointed by the leadership. Sherry believes that the committee should be taking "a leadership role" and that it has "a responsibility to make a decision." As she told me in a later interview:

> This is a private institution . . . a community we have chosen to join. I have no claim on this seat; I

asked and got the seat. Here I act more as an individual. . . . At the meeting I felt, "I can do this to you; if you don't like it, you can leave."

Ben responds by clarifying that he does not see the issue as primarily procedural, but educational:

In looking back at the process, we opted for change without realizing we had to catch them [the parents] up. Our decision was based on a lot of input. We didn't offer that educational process to the community, so they have been left behind. We need to educate them to the rightness of this decision or we will be in the terrible position of forcing them.

Don Marcus has his own perspective:

At the meeting there was no opportunity for rational discussion or articulation of the Jewish educational issues. Emotion crowded reason out of the room. . . . I don't want to over-react to blackmail statements. I hear them in relation to almost every decision that I and we make. . . . We are not promising people, "You can do anything you want to do." We get pounded on this. For example, with Bar Mitzvah we cannot guarantee any more a single Bar Mitzvah. All the emotional blackmail we get on that! Some of the criticism was valid. But I would hate to see us beat ourselves too hard.

The emotional outcry of these parents sounds all too familiar to Don: it reminds him of the outcry of those parents, so upset to learn their child will not be having a solo Bar or Bat Mitzvah, that they are ready to quit the temple. These threats are "blackmail statements" to be resisted. There were errors in procedure; but Don believes it is impossible to run a synagogue properly if committees like the RSC "beat [themselves] too hard" for making these small errors.

Ben is not convinced and persists in his argument.

"Good process allows people to adjust to change"; and, he adds, the committee has not yet done that on this issue. In part Don agrees: "Finally we need to accommodate people. We need to ask, are those the only two possibilities? To deal with the emotional charge we have to consider other possibilities."

The "other possibilities" include a proposal that Don offers. Let the committee be flexible as to when this new policy would come into effect. Let the affected families who already have children in the school be allowed to continue on course while new families joining the school after this year would be subject to the new policy. That would be a way of accommodating the protesting parents. But Don is resistant to the suggestion of holding an educational forum for these parents to discuss the reasons behind the change and to work through the emotional issues involved. Don believes that these issues are more productively handled through one-on-one conversations with the people involved.

Laura, who joined the meeting late and whose views carry a lot of weight on the committee, agrees with Don and Sherry:

> If we hold another meeting, will it be only those with vested interests who will come? Will it give the range of opinions that really exist? . . . We have to separate the process from the decision. The decision is sound and forgive us for the process errors. That is the most honest approach unless the committee thinks the decision is a mistake.

No one present thinks the decision was a mistake; no one wants to change it, for these members believe that Hebrew should be studied in a meaningful way by all the children. Yet Ben expresses his concern: "If we caused a lot of people to be incensed and alienated, it is no longer a curricular decision, but a matter of preserving the community." Laura responds to Ben's concern:

> Say that we think that we made the right deci-

sion, but to mitigate the impact on the individuals involved, we can put a process in place. . . . We could have educated people better, but still they would have been furious. With no challenge [in the RSC] to the decision, we should acknowledge our mistakes, correct what we can, but not by holding another open meeting.

Laura agrees with Don that education will not mitigate people's fury; the fury is a given of the situation. What can be done is to admit procedural errors, offer a process to correct the errors and stick by the decision. Don reinforces Laura's position by saying, "People are not really interested in the principles they articulated, but in their own situations." If those situations can be rectified by offering families already in the school the option of their children remaining in the school without having to take Hebrew, the outcry will die down and the new policy can go into effect for the families entering the school after this year.

The RSC, adopting Laura's proposal, agrees "not to reconsider their decision, but to be responsive" to the needs of the families already in the school. Don Marcus assures them this could be done. Those families already in the school will be grandfathered into the old arrangement of continuing religious education on Sundays alone. Don concludes that they thereby will be sending a message to the affected people: "We want and care for you and your children, but want to give you the best we have to offer." The best in the future will include a Hebrew education for each child; for now, accommodating the individuals involved would be the best way out of the committee's procedural dilemma.

What's at Stake?

I was fascinated by the debate within the RSC because it captured much of what Jewish educators and synagogue lay leaders need to think about when introducing change into a religious school curriculum.

The debate was primarily about how the RSC should understand and hence respond to the dissenting voices raised. No one disputed that the committee had made procedural errors that should be corrected. Ben saw the RSC as being accountable to the parents in the school, who are the committee's natural constituency. *Accountable* does not mean that the RSC should allow the parents to make this decision or that every family should be allowed to make policy for itself. Rather, the RSC has the responsibility to educate the parents as to the rationale for these changes and allow open debate so that people can work through the emotional issues that distress them. Ben expressed his belief that mandating Hebrew touches on deeper issues, including the attachment to the classical Reform tradition that some feel is under attack. He continued to worry that they will feel this decision is being forced on them, that they either have to send their children for Hebrew or be forced out of the temple.

Sherry, Laura, and Don acknowledged the need for the RSC to be responsive to parental input, but distinguished between being responsive and handing the decision over to parents who are far less informed than the committee about issues of educational policy. They also questioned what *being responsive* means in a situation in which the voices of dissent do not represent the majority of parents who send their children for a Hebrew education without complaint. In an open meeting the committee might have expected the protesting minority to be the dominating voice; but it would be a mistake to allow the shrillness of the minority protest to distract the committee from the rightness of its own decision: Let the decision stand because it makes educational sense; but let the committee be responsive by making accommodations for those individual families currently affected so they will not feel excluded from the temple community.

On the surface, the facts of the case seem to support this second argument. Even at the open meeting, of the thirty-five parents in attendance, only about ten were in vocal dissent. I spoke with several of the others who told me that they were surprised by the heat of the debate, but did not agree with the protesters. Yet they felt that they could not express their views because the heated emotional tone precluded their participation. My sense is that at the meeting itself, had the parents been polled, a majority of parents would have supported the change.

Nor could the RSC have honestly said at the meeting that they were seeking input on the decision itself. The RSC had followed Temple Akiba's standard procedure. They had studied the issue, voted on it, and sent their proposal to the Board of Trustees for its approval. The board had already approved this change in policy, and hence, the change in policy was officially already in effect by the time the open meeting took place. The meeting was therefore designed to explain the new policy to the parents rather than to explore whether it should take place. The committee could choose to hold more meetings of explanation or modify the decision in certain ways, but it was unlikely to go back to the board and ask for a reversal of the approved change.

Finally, who could expect controversial change to be implemented without resistance and protest? If the vehemence of the protest caught most by surprise, the presence of a protesting minority who used this format to loudly exclaim their unhappiness might be seen as an expected part of the change process. There was a ritual quality to the protest.[7] And Don was accurate in predicting that once the RSC agreed to make accommodations for individual families affected by the change, the whole issue of mandatory Hebrew would seem to fade away. With the exception of Janet, who raised this issue at a temple meeting a year after the event, I never again heard reference made to the controversy around mandatory Hebrew. The change in policy seemed to have been absorbed by the institution.

If the controversy proved short-lived, and the debate within the RSC seemed to be resolved by the facts of the case, why is this debate of interest? What is at stake here? I would contend that although on the surface the facts of the case point in one direction, beneath the surface the two sides within the RSC represent distinctly different views of how educational change ought to be carried out in a synagogue. Whereas in the short run the majority perspective proved effective, the questions that Ben raised about its long-term effectiveness are important to consider. Perhaps if we recast the "mandatory Hebrew" controversy as a social drama, it will be easier to see their importance.

"Mandatory Hebrew" As Social Drama

Recasting this controversy as a social drama requires that we first locate the breach in the normative structure that set the crisis in motion. We know the breach is located in the general culture of the congregation rather than in the details of the proposed change. Were the significance of "mandatory Hebrew" limited to the curriculum of the religious school, there is little chance that the RSC would have taken so long to make its decision or that their decision would have drawn the reaction that it did. Throughout this controversy there was little discussion of whether the school should be devoting so many hours to teaching Hebrew and virtually no questioning of the educational value of the Hebrew program. Rather, people's concerns focused on the symbolic and ideological overtones of making Hebrew *mandatory*.

Looking at the claims made by the protesting parents, we find they were protesting several different perceived breaches:

(a) the way the change was made;
(b) the intrusion of a mandatory requirement in a congregation that stresses the value of choice;
(c) the insistence that knowing Hebrew is essential to being an educated Jew; and
(d) the constriction of an atmosphere of welcome and inclusion.

Perhaps taken alone, none of these would have set off the protest. But taken together, these claims represented for the protesters a mighty breach in the value structure of Temple Akiba.

Had the RSC not called for an open meeting of parents to discuss the proposed change, the crisis may not have spread as rapidly. But once everyone was gathered together, each of the protesters could feed off the grievances of the others and feel an increasing sense of outrage over the violations committed by the RSC. When Sherry and Don each tried to assure the parents that the RSC had heard their concerns and would deal with them, they were shouted down. Trust had eroded, and the crisis was sizzling. Sitting there at the meeting, I was not sure at that point how this intense tension would be resolved. But Ben stepped in at that liminal moment, and with his words of empathy and humility began the process of redress. Perhaps his skill as an experienced therapist made a difference, but I could feel the high point of tension receding as Ben spoke. Then, almost miraculously, Sherry was able to bring this discussion to a close.

Turner is clear: bringing a discussion to conclusion is not the same as bringing a crisis to resolution. When the open meeting ended, I saw some of the protesting parents seek one another out to plan the next step. Don would receive three impassioned letters from parents who spoke up. The members of the RSC intuitively knew when they met again that the ball was in their court and that there was more reparative work to be accomplished. In fact, they devoted not one, but three meetings to work out these actions.

The debate within the RSC can now be recast as a disagreement over the appropriate reparative steps to be taken in a crisis like this. Don was arguing that two steps are needed:

(1) making the needed accommodations so that all those currently affected by this change will not feel they are being forced out of the community; and

(2) following up individually with the protesting parents who wrote to him so they will know that as their rabbi and educator, he still cares about them as individuals.

This second step represented for Don the final stage of the social drama: the rearrangement of social relations. He wanted to be sure that those relationships were not weakened, and may even be strengthened, as a result of the crisis.

Ben's notion of redress is more inclusive than Don's, and he sought to distinguish between accommodating people's immediate needs and addressing the fundamental questions raised by their protest. Surely accommodating their needs could cool off their protest, but would it also answer their basic questions? Would it bring them more deeply into the circle of the community or leave them as peripheral onlookers?

If this crisis is to be resolved in a way that also draws the protesting parents into the community's circle of trust, the leadership will have to act differently from the way that the majority suggests. The members of the RSC will have to extend their role to include helping those parents to understand why learning Hebrew has become so central to the synagogue's educational mission, for indeed, many Jews do not understand "why Hebrew?"

Ben explained his position more fully to me in a conversation we had later that spring. He based his views in part on the powerful, first meeting that he and his wife ever had with Don Marcus. It was at the time that they first were considering sending their child to this school.

> My wife came from a very Reform congregation and I came from a Conservative background, where I learned to read [Hebrew]. . . . Don was strongly recommending the Hebrew track. My wife, who had no Hebrew training, asked: Why bother? I always assumed you went to Hebrew school to learn Hebrew. That's part of a Jewish education. But I always felt ambivalent about it because it was just a matter of learning to read the prayers. Don talked about it and convinced my wife, who was leaning the other way, about the importance of it.

"Why bother?" is the question that needs to be addressed about studying Hebrew. Ben's wife grew up in a classical Reform congregation that taught her not to bother with Hebrew. Ben has his own ambivalent memories with which to contend. But Don, in Ben's words, "put us in touch with how much each of us had longed for a Jewish education that would be meaningful and tie together what the customs are really about." Don was able to convince them that Hebrew is a key to understanding the Jewish life that they would want their child to have.

Ben went on to say, "As a committee we have not done a good job in publicizing the reasons for mandatory Hebrew, and in that kind of vacuum, all kinds of misimpressions grow up." If Don can explain to Ben and his wife why Hebrew is such an essential part of a Jewish education, why has neither he nor the RSC done the job of educating the other parents so they too will grasp the rationale for this change?

I thought that this was an important enough question to pose directly to Don. In an interview which took place two years after these events, I posed the question and could tell Don took exception to it. He responded with feeling:

> Why indeed? Because the majority of the people about whom we are speaking are absent at every opportunity for information-gathering and exchange. . . . These aren't people who appear when there is a neutral base. They appear only after the fact when they discover that something is not to their liking. They have to be immediately and directly affected.

Don distinguished between the parents who came to the open meeting only to protest and the others who came to establish a dialogue. In Don's view, dialogue is the essential ground for educating parents and resolving a crisis.

To exemplify his point, Don spoke of the Webbers, a family faithful to classical Reform Judaism, who wrote him of their concerns after the open meeting.

With the Webber family there is real legitimacy to their being classical Reform Jews. They have sent three daughters to the school. . . . These parents have inherited an authentic classical Reform Judaism and are prepared to live it out. But there is not enough of them to have a community of classical Reform Jews. It just will not be around long. So what is my responsibility to these kids? I keep trying to articulate my position in relation to the kids and we have a positive relationship.

But when this [issue] got politicized [at the open meeting], . . . there wasn't any honesty. Hearing that, the Webbers did not know what to believe and wondered, "Is that what they are trying to do?"

It is not easy for Don to explain to the Webbers his view that classical Reform Judaism cannot insure the Jewish continuity of their children. But Don struggles to communicate this message in ways that still respect their integrity. He can do that only in a relationship of mutual trust and honesty. When the issue gets politicized, honesty is no longer possible, and education is replaced by political rhetoric that blocks the path to resolution.

At the RSC meetings, I heard Ben questioning this suspicion of the protesting parents. In a sense, he argued, these parents are asking for the same treatment that the RSC granted its own members. When there was serious division within the ranks of the RSC, the committee postponed making a decision to give everyone more time to think about the issues involved. These parents are now asking—albeit in very off-putting tones—for more time to discuss these issues in a public arena since earlier in the process they were excluded from participating. Ben was suggesting that taking this next step in educating parents may also be part of the RSC's leadership role.

Resolution involves helping people to work through their feelings about these issues and changes. Perhaps in talking about the feelings of exclusion and alienation, people could begin to separate out those feelings from the issue of Hebrew in the school. Perhaps in feeling that their concerns were being heard and understood, they would feel less belligerent and more open to discussing the educational questions with more detachment. The highly emotional tone of the open meeting may have had as much to do with the way the RSC set up the process as with the strong feelings that these parents brought to the discussion.

But the majority within the RSC did not believe that these kinds of questions can be effectively discussed in a public form, and this debate itself came to no resolution. The majority position was followed, Ben held to his view, and I was left wondering why Ben's view carried so little weight. In subsequent conversations, Don tried to show me that Ben's position was unrealistic within the context of Temple Akiba. The temple's governance structure did not allow for this type of educational process. In "an environment in which there has been no experience of it," Don claimed, the RSC could not simply begin to educate in the public way that Ben advocated. While Ben's position is theoretically convincing, it is not realizable within the current structure of Temple Akiba. The only realistic remedy in Don's view is to increase the opportunities for one-to-one dialogue between the parents and the educational professionals in the synagogue.

I do not doubt Don Marcus' realistic assessment of the governance structure of Temple Akiba. There is an impersonal edge to the way business is conducted by the board and its committees. But I also continue to see in Ben's position a greater appreciation for the educational value of social drama. The drama contains lessons for all involved. Of course, it is very painful to face angry protest against one's own decision. Of course, the protesters may not be right in all the claims they make. But still, as Turner and Myerhoff have taught, the social drama reflects back to us the divisions in our midst and the conflicts that we as a community cannot easily resolve. The drama also allows us to define ourselves by enacting those values that we consider primary.

There is no doubt that the foremost value for which the RSC stood firm was the synagogue's commitment to provide all its children with a quality Jewish education.

Given the "distinctive Torah" that the rabbis have been teaching and the educational approach that Temple Akiba has adopted, Hebrew has become a core value of the curriculum. Tested by the fire of protest, the RSC made accommodations to the protesting parents, but affirmed through dramatic action their and the board's commitment to this core value.

The social drama left unresolved a key conflict within the culture of this synagogue. It is the very same conflict raised by Marcia at the family education session. Can Temple Akiba embrace a more traditional approach to Judaism and at the same time still remain open to a diverse population of Jews who expect affirmation for their contemporary values and lifestyles?

Don Marcus: Providing Something of Substance

How the temple can balance the values of being inclusive and providing Jewish substance was an issue very much on the mind of Don Marcus. It first came up in our conversations in an interview in November, when, for the first time, Don told me about the proposed "mandatory Hebrew" policy. He was explaining why he had raised this issue with the RSC.

> I wonder if we are providing kids who are here only on Sunday with something of substance. I am not sure we are. Given that every alternative is available, I wanted [the RSC] to think about what we should stand for as a community. A message is communicated when you offer so many options that it is not clear what is your primary goal. . . . If beyond a desire to be inclusive, you want the kid to get something, I am not sure we can provide it [on Sunday alone].

To be effective, Don believes, education has to have clear primary goals. His primary goals in the school are for each child to be substantively engaged with Jewish tradition and to develop an attachment to the synagogue community that will last beyond Bar or Bat Mitzvah. In his view, a Sunday school education cannot lead to either goal. It does not provide enough substantive Jewish knowledge for children to become engaged with tradition or enough time on site to develop any lasting attachments to the people in the school. Therefore "beyond a desire to be inclusive," the Sunday option is an educational failure that should be eliminated.

Don has been a major proponent of building an inclusive community in the synagogue. Yet he is saying that inclusiveness should not come at the cost of what is primary: providing Jewish substance. At the March meeting of the RSC, Don returned to this position when he spoke about the leadership that this committee should exert.

> I have a bias. I believe that we as a committee must establish the program that *we* recommend. We should invite everyone to join that program, but not let the least common denominator dictate our priorities. That is what leadership should do: not be embarrassed, but be flexible.

He underlined his message: in an inclusive community there needs to be standards set by the leadership. The standards should be set flexibly, but without embarrassment. The alternative, of being purely flexible and inclusive, would lead to everyone's doing whatever they please and a congregation's not having clear standards.

This juxtaposition between inclusiveness and standards was made again by Don in perhaps his most public statement of the year, his Yom Kippur sermon. In the sermon he made reference to the recently released National Jewish Population Study,[8] which highlighted the continuing increase in the percentage of Jews who are marrying out of their faith. Rabbi Marcus took the position that the problems of Jewish continuity are evident in everyone's lives and cannot be reduced to the single issue of intermarriage. Then he spoke directly of what the synagogue should do for "the interfaith families with children who are uncertain whether to choose a religious identity for the family."

> These couples are unprepared to dive into the waters of Jewish life. It is incumbent upon us to make the pool inviting with no exception other than the hope that they will choose to test the water. . . .
> We must discover a way to communicate that this house is a safe place for their discovery of their identity. We must not, however, do so at the expense of our normative programs. These must not be diluted; the establishment of standards and expectations is critical if we would reverse the trends.

Don called for making this house of worship a safe place for interfaith families. Yet he inserted an essential caution: "We must not do so at the expense of our normative programs." The most open welcome to the currently unaffiliated needs to be balanced by "the establishment of standards and expectations." Don was fighting a tendency to equate openness with a dilution of Jewish substance.

Don Marcus: A Retrospective Perspective

Two years later, Don and I had one more occasion to review the questions raised by the "mandatory Hebrew" controversy and his Yom Kippur sermon. It was clear Don had continued to think about these questions and saw matters somewhat differently from how he saw them during the crisis itself.

In retrospect, Don had no regrets about ending the Sunday school, but now sees that the debate about its closing left a void. Missing from the RSC's deliberations was a discussion of how developing normative standards could be balanced by developing the alternative side—of openness and inclusiveness. A congregation like Temple Akiba that wishes to welcome a diversity of Jews needs to be constantly working on new ways to bring them to Judaism. It needs to create new ways of learning and experiencing Judaism that will work for a diversity of family situations. Don thinks that his Yom Kippur sermon touched on that theme but that there was little articulation of the theme during the "mandatory Hebrew" controversy.

Don now suggests that the thinking of all the parties (including himself) in the "mandatory Hebrew" controversy was limited by certain assumptions. The debate assumed an either/or conflict. One was either for greater Hebrew or greater inclusiveness. But to polarize *Hebrew* and *inclusiveness* is to draw a false dichotomy. The congregation does not have to choose between these values, for they are actually mutually dependent on one another. In fact, *the only way that Temple Akiba can risk being truly inclusive is by assuring that its core is more authentically Jewish. But if Temple Akiba focuses too exclusively on its Jewish core, it will cease to be true to its mission of serving modern Jews in a changing world.*

To rephrase Don's insight, classical Reform Judaism could afford in its time to do away with more traditional elements of Judaism because it could assume a stable and homogeneous Jewish population. But operating today in a far more diverse Jewish community, Temple Akiba needs to embrace more traditional elements of Judaism *in order to* open its doors to this diversity. It needs the Hebrew and the other Judaic elements to signify its Jewishness at a time when its population alone no longer assures that continuity. Were this new traditionalism to shut off the access of the diverse populations, then, in Don's view, Temple Akiba would no longer be true to its mandate of serving the Jews on the borders of the community—hence the interdependent relationship. Adopting more elements of traditional Judaism anchors the congregation so that it can absorb new populations, and the inclusiveness assures that a more traditional congregation will not lose sight of its basic mission of serving a diversity of Jews.

Final Thoughts

The "mandatory Hebrew" controversy has opened a

deeper view of the tensions created by Temple Akiba's responsiveness to both the normative claims of the Jewish tradition and the pressing claims of a changing Jewish community. From the start, the RSC weighed how to balance raising the standards of Hebrew learning for all students with the congregation's policy of including a broad diversity of families within the temple community. This case once again demonstrates this is not an easy balance to maintain.

Maintaining a creative balance between the claims of tradition and the demands of modernity requires seeing both sides as dynamic and evolving. The meaning of *tradition* is constantly evolving, as are the educational programs needed to teach tradition within the school curriculum. The populations whom the synagogue is serving keep changing, as do the programs needed to draw these people into the synagogue community. The claims from both sides need to be honored. When one side is perceived as having gotten the upper hand, the other side is sure to respond in protest. That is what happened with "mandatory Hebrew." Knowing how to respond to the protest and knowing how to restore the balance between the contending sides are crucial leadership skills needed to manage the change process within synagogue life.

Chapter 6

Synagogue Drama and Education

I began this research project with one question and ended it with another. The first question emerged from reading Schoem's ethnography and the many other studies that found synagogue education seriously lacking. I wanted to know: Could I find an alternative? Are there any synagogue schools that do provide a quality Jewish education? Are there any synagogues that offer their schools the kinds of support that make it feasible for them to provide a quality Jewish education to their students and their families?

I have not found an educational miracle at Temple Akiba, but I have tried to show through this ethnography that an alternative to what David Schoem described does exist. Readers may debate how "good" the Jewish education described in this school is, but I am convinced that the differences between Temple Akiba and Schoem's Shalom Synagogue are real enough to make a difference. Of course, without any long-term measures, I can base that judgment only on the observed data offered in his study and mine.

I acknowledge that much of this difference can be attributed to the educational leadership provided by the two rabbis, Norman Davidman and Don Marcus. But it goes beyond their exceptional team leadership. For Temple Akiba has made Jewish education—within a Reform context—a priority for their congregation for most of this century. There is some quality in the culture of this type of congregation that sets it apart as an educating synagogue.

I have tried to show that a synagogue's making Jewish education a priority is not simply a statement about teaching the children. I began this study with an examination of the Shabbat-morning Torah study group as a way of indicating that serious Jewish education has to begin with the adults. Rabbis and educators who have a "distinctive Torah" to teach adult members are more likely to design quality education for the children as well. Rabbis and educators who lack that vision also have less quality to offer their congregation's children and youth.

I recognize that there are severe limits to how generalizable any of these claims can be. My aim in this ethnography is to show the *possibilities for synagogue education* and leave others to follow up on this one case. I suggest that it would be important to explore what can be achieved educationally in other synagogues if the leadership and the parent body are united in believing that a "distinctive Torah" can be taught in their community.[1]

My second question arose from exploring the dialogue that takes place between the educational professionals and the parents and children around issues of religious significance. I came into this study assuming that there would be cultural tensions between the religious message of synagogue education and the more secular perspectives that both parents and children bring with them into the synagogue. I expected debate and disagreement, but discovered a deeper and more delicate tension than anticipated.

As a participant in this synagogue culture, I was drawn to those moments when Jewish learning would be proceeding along in an orderly fashion and, quite suddenly, be disrupted by unanticipated tension. I began to visualize these moments as "mini-earthquakes," in which a rising, underground tension would erupt and a fault would appear in the smooth surface of the lesson. As participant-observer I would want to peer into the fault to discover both why the surface cracked and what was pushing up from below.

Turner and Myerhoff have both been my guides in seeing these moments through the lens of social drama. Together with Heilman, they have set me exploring the role of social drama and cultural performances in the educating synagogue. I have come to believe that these crises, in spite of all their inherent dangers, also provide rare opportunities for educational growth for those who grasp their significance.

A Dramatic Perspective on Synagogue Life

The previous chapters have pointed to issues and moments that emerged as "dramatic" during this study. There were the obvious cases, like the "mandatory Hebrew" controversy, and the less obvious ones, like Barbara's teaching Jonah to the seventh grade. Her switching frames set off a conflict that came to the fore in dramatic fashion. A quiet crisis needed to be resolved by ending the discussion and respecting the students' limits.

In calling these varied moments "dramatic," I am clearly departing from common usage and referring instead to the usage suggested by Turner, Myerhoff, and Heilman. I am describing these moments as "social dramas" and suggesting they have special significance in teaching us about the educating synagogue.

Before reconsidering these specific moments, I want to raise the broader question of why I have taken this dramatic perspective on synagogue life. I have made a preliminary case for this move in Chapter 1. A recent book by Jack Wertheimer, *A People Divided: Judaism in Contemporary America*, offers more extensive background for explaining my choice.[2]

Wertheimer argues that American Judaism, in parallel to American Christianity, has been moving over the past twenty-five to thirty years in varied ideological directions. During the 1950s and early 1960s there was a time of greater ideological coherence within these religious communities, but that coherence seems to have splintered since the late 1960s. Some religious communities, such as Orthodox Jews and fundamentalist Christians, have moved primarily to the right on both theological and political fronts. Other communities, such as Reform Judaism and mainline Protestantism, have moved primarily to the left on those same fronts. Other communities, such as Conservative

Judaism and the American Catholic Church, have been split by factions that have moved towards the right and the left.[3]

Movement towards the right or left masks some vital countertrends, as can be seen from the examples of the Orthodox and Reform movements. A move towards the right for the Orthodox features an increased rejection of modernism and an attempt to build a separate world to protect the faithful from excessive contact with the "unholy" spheres of modern life. Yet, these same movements—such as Chabad Hasidism, that attempts to wait out the modern world—have become increasingly adept at using modern technologies to communicate their message to both the faithful and the secular worlds. They have become more involved with contemporary politics, in the United States and Israel, in the name of protecting the "holy" from the "profane." And as they aim to reject the norms of modern life, they attract the attention of the public media, who show an increasing fascination with these variations on modern life.[4]

The Reform movement has moved to the left on issues like feminism, outreach to interfaith families, and inclusion of gay Jews within the community. Yet, as we have seen, many Reform congregations have also moved to embrace more traditional elements of Judaism, including introducing services such as *Seliḥot* and practices such as sitting *shivah* during the mourning period. Reform Jews have also moved away from certain stances that they once took in relation to the broader culture. When the Orthodox began Jewish day schools in the 1940s and 1950s, the Reform community objected to this as a form of parochialism and used those occasions to restate their firm commitment to the public schools. But by the 1980s the Reform movement began opening their own day schools. There was still protest from the "anti-parochialists," but day schools received approval from the Reform movement in 1985. The Reform move to the left has taken place within a context of increased absorption with Jewish tradition and increased distance from the universalistic agenda of classical Reform Judaism.

In Wertheimer's view, this moving in multiple directions opens up certain advantages, but it also creates certain problems:

> Whereas Reform was formerly a movement that on principle said no to some aspects of Jewish tradition, it is now a movement that is open to all Jewish possibilities, whether traditional or innovative. . . . The result is a Judaism open to all options and therefore appealing to a broad range of Jews. . . . The dilemma this raises for the Reform movement is one of limits, of boundaries. If the autonomy of the individual prevails above all else, what beliefs and practices unite all Reform Jews? (p.96)

Orthodox Judaism has long had—and has recently stressed—reliance on the authority of the rabbi to set the tone and the halakhic standards for the community. That system creates the problem of intense rivalries among rabbis and between communities. In the Reform movement the rabbi is not a *posek*, a decisive voice. Yet, rabbis like Norman Davidman and Don Marcus have attempted to point in a direction and articulate a rationale for the mission they envision. Although their direction is galvanizing to many in the congregation, it is hardly the final word, however.

Theirs cannot be the final word, for Reform is a Judaism of choice. Since the voice of tradition has no veto over the voice of individual conscience, the rabbis may lead but not dictate policy. In congregations like Temple Akiba, where there are so many different understandings of what the key values are, how in the absence of a *posek* does a consensus develop? How does the congregation determine which of "all Jewish possibilities, traditional or innovative" to call their own and which to rule out as not their own?

In practice certain common understandings do develop. Certain issues, such as officiating at intermarriages, are left to rabbinic decision. Other issues, such as curriculum for the school, are decided primarily by the professionals in consultation with a lay committee. Others, such as mourning practices, are left to individual choice in consultation with the clergy. But there are the issues over which there is real contest, when the rabbis and educators may suggest a direction, but when there is significant precedent and opinion in other directions. How in these particular cases of lack of consensus does a decision get made?

There is no one answer to this question. There are occasions when indecision, postponed decision, or simple vagueness rules the day. There are other times when allowing multiple options to be followed works well enough.[5] There are also times, and these are of special interest, when one or both sides decides to push for taking a stand to replace the vagueness or multiple options. The push itself is perceived as breaking with established norms and often results in a crisis developing within the organization. It is when this occurs that Turner's social drama enters the picture.

Turner is not describing any fissure within an organization in which two sides stand off against each other in a struggle for power. His interest, like mine, is limited to those conflicts in which the social conflict is built upon and reflects a fault line in the basic values of the organization. At such times each side of the conflict feels that it knows it is right because its arguments are based on values central to the organization. Thus neither side is challenging the value structure; both sides are claiming, with justification, to represent that very value structure. The dilemma is that the organization has embraced different values which at times conflict with one another.

In the case of implementing mandatory Hebrew at Temple Akiba, the term *mandatory* flew in the face of the basic Reform principle of choice and autonomy. As long as everyone had an educational option to choose, no conflict developed over the Hebrew program. But once the religious school committee proposed to do away with the Sunday school option and to require all students to study Hebrew during the week, the champions of choice cried foul. The RSC was violating the principle of choice.

For its part, the RSC had an equal claim on the value agenda of Temple Akiba. For many decades, the temple

has been devoted to excellence in Reform Jewish education. If excellence in Jewish education is now thought to
require students to attain significant knowledge of Hebrew, then how could the RSC in good conscience continue
to allow for the non-Hebrew Sunday school option? The
values of education and choice were in conflict.

Turner shows how once a social drama emerges, it follows several steps towards resolution. In terms of the crisis
of mandatory Hebrew, those steps have been described
here. I have also followed Myerhoff's suggestions that certain social dramas can also function as *definitional ceremonies*. These dramas become definitional in the sense of
providing the group with the opportunity to enact or perform their basic values in the face of challenges. In the case
of mandatory Hebrew, had the parents not challenged the
RSC's decision and forced the RSC members to wrestle
with the questions of choice in relation to quality Jewish
education, the members would never have known how
strongly they had invested in the value of Hebrew. Further,
their standing up for the importance of these values gave
greater definition to their work as a committee and
attracted the support of the board. These consequences, in
turn, resulted in putting the temple more squarely on the
side of a Hebrew-based education.

In the midst of the debate over mandatory Hebrew,
one of the protesting parents expressed anguish that this
decision could lead to excluding certain families from the
temple. In response, Don argued that a synagogue cannot
be all things to all people. Were Temple Akiba to allow
anyone who joined to design the educational or religious
program that simply fit *their* family's needs best, the synagogue would lose all definition. It would cease to be a
viable organization, with boundaries, limits, and directions. At some point the synagogue has to define itself,
even at the cost of some members feeling excluded.

Myerhoff would underline *the act of definition*. Collective identities may be ascribed to an institution from the
outside. But the key to a vital organization is its members'
activeness in defining and redefining that collective identity for themselves. Such defining cannot come from one

deliberative act alone; rather, the evolving definition has to be performed or enacted. It can be performed in social and ritual actions. And, some of the clearest moments of collective self-definition come in the face of challenge and crisis.

Myerhoff's point brings me back to Wertheimer's book. Wertheimer's portrayal of contemporary Reform Judaism would suggest a movement that has given up some of its historical self-definition in order to respond to changing times and to accommodate a variety of differing ideological positions. This move has paid dividends in enlarging the tent and including increasing numbers of American Jews under the banner of Reform.[6] But the move has its costs in terms of coherence. It becomes harder under these circumstances to say what belongs within the movement and what is beyond the pale.

If the Reform movement, or much of American Judaism, is to gain coherence, much of the work has to take place on the congregational level where most committed Jews are involved. Myerhoff has suggested that for a center or synagogue, gaining coherence cannot come easily. It is no longer possible to rely solely on the rabbis or the board of trustees to offer coherence through sermons, proclamations, or closet decisions. Coherence or self-definition is gained, if at all, in the field of action. In one corner of this field stands the stage of enacted conflict. At times congregations have to be willing to risk the damage of conflict to gain the benefits of coherence.

That, I would claim, is the special role of social drama in the study of contemporary synagogues. The social drama allows the ethnographer to observe the congregation in the act of collective self-definition. As defining ceremonies, these dramas are enactments of the limits and boundaries that Wertheimer has questioned. They are the congregation's way of discovering—and the ethnographer's way of observing—the values that more deeply animate the life of the synagogue. They are not the only way of performing values or enacting limits; this comes through social and ritual actions as well. But social dramas are one sure mirror of the evolving identity of the congregation.

Social Drama and Education

I have argued that social dramas are powerful vehicles for educating their participants to see more clearly the values that animate synagogue life. In the family education session, presented in Chapter 2, recall how attentively the parents and children listened as Rabbi Marcus was describing the rationale for the rituals of mourning. In retrospect we can see that those parents—sitting next to their children and caught up in the emotions aroused by the session—were performing as Jewishly as they could. But when the children were safely upstairs in their classrooms and the parents were asked to evaluate the session critically, they switched to perform their roles as *liberal* Jews. They rallied to Marcia's call and insisted on the full inclusion of nontraditional families within the circle of Jewish ritual.

I have little doubt there was a hint of rebellion against the rabbi. Having offered the rabbi their love and reverence, it is not surprising that they would come around from the other side and attack him as a traditionalist. The relationship with the rabbi is inevitably filled with ambivalence.[7]

Beyond rebellion, there were lessons offered by the social drama that could not be learned in the family education session. They learned that Don Marcus will stand by the tradition even when pushed hard. They learned that there is more to Reform Judaism than political correctness, but also that in doing his rabbinic work of burying the dead and comforting the mourners, Don will stretch his understandings of tradition to take into full account their lives and those of their family. This is not the idealized rabbi of the first session; but it is a rabbi who is working hard to synthesize his reading of Jewish tradition with his understanding of contemporary life.

I call these "lessons" even though they do not come out of a book or from a lecture with questions and answers. By emerging from a social drama, they may have a meaning deeper than those learned from a book or lecture. As Myerhoff and Heilman suggest, they may be more credible for having been performed in the face of conflict and not simply taught from the front of the room.

Drama and Belief

A drama of a different sort was performed in Barbara's seventh-grade class as reported in Chapter 4. Barbara and her students were engaged in a spirited discussion of the first chapter in the Book of Jonah that involved an examination of God's motives for sending the prophet Jonah to the unrepentant city of Nineveh. "Why does God care about them?" asked Andrew. "They don't even believe in God."

As a skilled teacher, Barbara did not try to answer these questions herself, but to engage the students in thinking about them. They were pleased to do so and came up with a variety of perspectives on the relationship between God and Jonah. But one response stands out. Responding to why Jonah would be reluctant to go to Nineveh, Rebekka suggested, "Maybe Jonah didn't know [this was God speaking]. If God spoke to you, you'd think you were crazy."

To this note of skepticism Barbara directly addressed herself. This text "was written a long time ago. We have records of people saying that God spoke to them, and we are not sure what they meant." Barbara included everyone present in the "we" who "are not sure what they [in those days] meant." Yet she did not directly doubt that "they" did speak meaningfully in reporting "God spoke to them."

Had Barbara left off at this point, I think Rebekka would have been satisfied and the discussion of Jonah would have continued. Instead Barbara took a risk. She asked: "What would you say today that might be like God's speaking to you? Did you ever do something that you feel fits in with what God says?"

Barbara took another step. She told her students that when she listens to music she sometimes feels closer to God and that when she climbs a mountain she also sometimes has that feeling. But no one else in the class said that they share that feeling. Finally, Staci stated the objection,

"Not God. I don't believe in God. It is something else, but not God."

Barbara tried no more. She heard the silence and Staci's objection and immediately shifted gears—no rebuttal to Staci, no probing of other students. Barbara immediately brought the focus back to Jonah and closed the lesson.

Barbara's risk-taking constituted a break from the normative order. Here was a safe and distanced discussion of the prophet Jonah. In that context, questions about God felt appropriate. Students could freely talk about God as a character in the narrative and not feel personally implicated by the discussion. But once Barbara broke rank with that normative frame and brought up how she experiences God in the present, the distance was suspended. Even worse, once she asked the students to share experiences of God in their life, the conversation got too close for comfort. This move set off a classroom crisis.

Every step of the way the students were trying to warn Barbara. First there was the silence. Then Rebekka offered that she had "never had a conversation with God." Then Debby explained that while she feels good when she climbs a mountain, "it is like a good accomplishment." But finally Staci stated the objection explicitly: "Not God. I don't believe in God."

At that crucial moment Barbara took the corrective action of ending the discussion. I have wondered what would have happened had she pushed on. What if she had taken even mild offense at Staci's statement and become personally defensive? What if she had thought it necessary to defend the faith? I think the answer is clear. The crisis would have spread, the students would have tuned out, fought back, or simply misbehaved. We have all been in classes where that has happened.[8]

But why didn't Barbara stand her ground the way Don Marcus did with the parents in family education? I think the difference in her response results from the subtle distinction between these two dramas. In Don's case a statement he had made earlier about tradition was being called into question. He chose not to retract what he had said, but to maintain the integrity of the tradition as separate from the demands of modernity. But Don was not dealing directly with the parents' beliefs.

In Barbara's case, when Rebekka called it "crazy" to believe that God could speak to a human, Barbara made a move similar to Don's and defended the integrity of the biblical claim by claiming it to be separate from our cultural assumptions. But once she began exploring with the students the delicate area of personal belief, she was probing to see if the students could connect to an experience of God. When they made it clear that they would not demonstrate this connection, she chose to let the matter drop. Any further probing would have been intrusive—not a defense of tradition, but a violation of the principle of autonomy that governs these discussions at Temple Akiba.

Was anything learned from the drama in Barbara's class? I think so. The students used the dramatic occasions to define the limits of the classroom discussion: this is how far they will go in discussing God, and no further. Barbara used the drama to display a faith position different from the students' as well as a remarkable sensitivity to their boundaries. Although she probed the limits of their tolerance, once they set the limits, she was immediately respectful.

There was a reward for Barbara's display of respect: the students' trust. These students let Barbara know what is and is not on their minds, but without rebelling or acting out. When later in the school year they lost their enthusiasm for the close reading of Jonah, they asked if they could spend more time with modern, spoken Hebrew. Barbara heard the message. The results was the class' preparing a small-scale performance of Cinderella in Hebrew. This performance, staged on the last day of school for the lower grades, teachers, and clergy, was a joyous celebration of the Hebrew program. The other students and teachers were aglow with enthusiastic cheer.

After taking their bows, the seventh-grade students brought Barbara, the playwright, "on stage" for her applause. Here, I thought, was a testimony that all could behold of the relationship she had developed with this post–Bar and Bat Mitzvah class. Barbara, who has mastered the art of social drama, was being applauded on stage for her skills as a playwright. It doesn't get much sweeter than this in Hebrew school.

Social Drama and Leadership

Although Turner has charted the several steps in the unfolding of the social drama, he also makes it clear that the outcome to any given drama is unpredictable. These episodes have their liminal moments, when the drama could go either way: moving the organization towards either greater social reintegration or schism. Which way the drama plays out has much to do with the structure of the organization, but also with the moves made by the participants in the drama.[9]

In describing the social dramas at Temple Akiba, I am struck by the key role that the leadership plays as participants in the drama. Social dramas are times of testing not only the social integration of the organization but also the skills of the leadership in handling these crises.

In the family education session, it was Don who "inadvertently" set off the crisis by his remarks on who—according to traditional Judaism—are counted as primary mourners. Once he came under attack from Marcia and the other parents, his leadership skills were being tested. Could he stand his ground and still hold onto his relationship with this rebellious group? Don managed this by simultaneously defending the integrity of tradition and showing how he, as a modern rabbi, works flexibly with the tradition to meet the varied emotional and social needs of the mourning families. His reparative "concession" was to admit that in practice all the families stand within the circle of temple ritual. This move capped the crisis and allowed the parents to return to the original agenda of the meeting: evaluating the family education session.

But even with the crisis in check, the social drama was not yet over. Don left the meeting very upset. He decided to call Marcia, ask her what was bothering her, and offer to meet with her. These were very important steps in social reintegration. As he would later tell me, Don made clear to

Marcia that although he was hurt, he wanted to continue their relationship. Marcia took up his offer, shared some of her personal turmoil with Don, and their relationship was strengthened rather than weakened by the drama.

It is the leader's capacity to hold onto the relationship with those on the other side of the dramatic contest that I find so impressive and important. Both Don, in this case, and Barbara, in her Hebrew class, display the ability to be involved in the drama while staying apart from the emotional dynamics sufficiently to offer redress within the crisis and work towards social reintegration after the crisis has abated. The reintegrative move involves showing respect and making concessions to the claims of the other side. This move also involves holding on through the crisis to what is positive and shared in the relationship. Holding on may allow those who were so clearly divided by the crisis to become socially reintegrated with the resolution of the drama.[10]

There is an additional task for the leadership: learning from the drama itself. There are lessons to be learned from participating in the acts of self-definition. Barbara learned something about her seventh-grade class and was able to handle their next act of self-definition—"we want to be learning more spoken Hebrew"—with grace and accommodation. Don learned something from Marcia about interpreting or "reading" certain parental attacks on the rabbi as calls for help. He ended our subsequent conversation on this incident by saying, "You'll never know what will walk through the door here." I had the feeling he was more prepared for that eventuality than he was before.

Perhaps because I admired Don's handling of the crisis with Marcia, I was taken aback by his reaction one month later to the protesting parents at the open meeting on mandatory Hebrew. As he readily admitted to me, some of those parents got under his skin. They made him angry in a way that Marcia did not. Marcia was an involved parent who had developed a prior relationship with Don. Some of the protesting parents "came in off the streets" to launch this protest. Being people with whom Don had no relationship changed the dynamics of the situation for him.

Looking back at the open meeting, it was Ben, not Don, who provided the key reintegrative move. It was Ben who showed the respect for their position and allowed the concession that the RSC was yet an "adolescent committee" that could have made a mistake. His concession allowed the immediate crisis to abate and the meeting to go on to its next agenda item.

In the subsequent meetings of the RSC, Ben and his supporter favored increasing the outreach to all the protesting parents and educating them on the rationale for this change in policy. That strategy would go beyond concrete redress to bringing the RSC and the protesters back into one circle of conversation.

Don firmly opposed Ben's suggested move, for he did not believe it could be effective. Following the crisis with Marcia, he believed that effective social realigning requires one-on-one contact. With those parents who had written to him, he was anxious to establish dialogue. But he thought the others had no interest in conversation, only in protest. And who knows if he was incorrect in this judgment? As a result, this social drama ended differently from how the other two did. Although it defined more clearly the centrality of Hebrew to Temple Akiba's educational agenda, it did not bring any visible social realignment. Those who voiced a sense of being excluded, with some individual exceptions, were left feeling excluded. There was little healing of the wounds that were on display during the open meeting.

As a leader, however, Don did learn from the crisis. This became evident in his retrospective interview. Two years after the drama, Don could see what was not as clear to him at the time. In holding firm to the "mandatory Hebrew" agenda, Don and the RSC were able to place Hebrew—and all that it represented—more prominently on the synagogue's educational agenda. But they did not provide the same definitional focus for the outreach agenda of the synagogue. They closed the Sunday school without providing an option for attracting and educating those families who were not ready to buy into a three-days-a week school program.

Two years later Don was considering how to preserve the integrity of the school program and yet serve the needs of these other families. Don had learned, once again, that it is not enough to provide definition for the traditional agenda of Hebrew without also addressing the modernist agenda of outreach to the spectrum of contemporary families. Removed from the heat of the drama, Don kept working on the questions raised by the "mandatory Hebrew" controversy until he was satisfied he could provide an adequate educational response. In that sense, the social drama lasted in effect long after the crisis itself had abated.

Religion-in-the-Making

> These dramas are religion-in-the-making, for in them the Center people are agreeing upon and making authoritative the essential ideas that define them. . . . Always, self and society are known—to the subjects themselves and to the witnessing audience—through enactments. Rituals and ceremonies are cultural mirrors, opportunities for presenting collective knowledge. (Myerhoff, p. 32)

In synagogue life, social dramas are not the only or primary means available for the congregation to do the work of collective self-definition. The more common opportunity comes through the enactments of rituals and ceremonies. These do double work: they fulfill spiritual needs while also expressing the identity of those congregants who meaningfully participate in them.

I remember sitting at a Shabbat morning service at Temple Akiba on a brilliant fall morning during the festival of Sukkot. The services were being led by Rabbi Abeles, Rabbi Davidman, and Cantor Perry. After the ark was opened and the Torah scrolls were taken out to be read, there was a pause in the service for a baby naming. Rabbi Abeles, in her colorful *tallit*, led the naming ceremony.

The parents brought the infant up to the *bimah*. Rachel awaited them and guided them to a structure that looks like a *sukkah*. Under the *sukkah* Rachel recited the prayer for naming a girl child. The girl was named Jessica in English and *Sh'lomit* in Hebrew. Rachel then kissed the crying baby and the ceremony was complete. The parents and their new child descended from the *bimah* and the Torah reading began.

Remembering this naming service, I imagine that among the guests of the family are two retired rabbis, men in their seventies, the great-uncles of the infant Jessica. One is a classical Reform rabbi; the other, a traditional Conservative rabbi. Each is reacting to the ceremony he has just witnessed.

Uncle Sam, the traditionalist, is thinking he is very glad that his great-niece was named in the synagogue and given a beautiful Hebrew name; but this certainly was a strange naming service. First, there was the woman rabbi. All of his colleagues were male. Second, they did this naming before the Torah reading. In his synagogue, it is done when the father is called for an *aliyah*. And that is the next point. Traditionally, it is the father's (not both parents') role to name the daughter. Finally, what was that *sukkah* doing up on the *bimah*. Don't they know a *sukkah* belongs outdoors?[11]

Maurice, the classical Reform uncle, is thinking he is very glad that his great-niece was named in the temple; but was this a Reform naming ceremony? Jessica is such a beautiful name, with roots in the Bible. Why have a second, Hebrew, name? Will anyone call this child Sh'lomit? And, yes he knows these days women are rabbis. But that colorful *tallit?* And kissing the baby? Doesn't the rabbi realize that these excesses reduce the dignity of the service? Finally, that *sukkah* on the pulpit! Is that really necessary? There could be some lovely readings in the service to indicate that this is Sukkot. Why the need to incorporate all these ancient rituals? They have taken their traditionalism too far.

I imagine these internal monologues as a way of thinking about religion-in-the-making at Temple Akiba. This naming ceremony was recognizable to both uncles, yet decidedly different from what they had expected. It is too "traditional" from a classical Reform perspective. It could never have taken place in this form a generation or two earlier at Temple Akiba. Yet, it is markedly "modern" in relation to a traditional naming ceremony and could never have taken place at certain Conservative or any Orthodox synagogues. This ceremony is out of the ordinary from both of these perspectives precisely because it reflects with fair accuracy the Judaism practiced today at Temple Akiba. This baby naming bears the signs of being fashioned to fit the key values of this religious context.

Like social dramas, rituals and ceremonies express basic, collective values. *How* a congregation names an infant tells a lot about *what* the congregation values. To the discomfort of both these great-uncles, this naming ceremony accomplishes more than welcoming baby Jessica into the community. It also holds up a mirror to how this particular Jewish community sees itself. They see themselves as egalitarian in relation to gender; involving of congregants in lifecycle rituals; encouraging of Hebrew usage; comfortable with ancient religious symbols; and ready to touch, hug, or kiss as a way of conveying warmth and connection within the congregation. Moreover, the mirror images educate: they announce and point to the Judaism that the members are called to practice.

As Myerhoff concedes, "these reflections are not always accurate." Temple Akiba is not as warm a community as this ceremony suggests. The use of Hebrew names is inconsistent in the school. There are certain ancient Jewish symbols which never make their appearance on the *bimah*. Perfect gender equality does not yet exist at Temple Akiba. Yet, "more like myths than photographs," these rituals are "means employed to 'see' themselves" (p. 32). They hold up an image of Temple Akiba as its clergy would like it to be seen. They are the ideal images to be achieved.

Having been fashioned to reflect their context, do these rituals have the lasting power to be powerfully didactic to the witnessing audience? Is the fact that this ceremony was fashioned to reflect American Reform Judaism of the 1990s—a liberal religious tradition that by its nature changes with time—limit its educational impact?

Or does the resonance with current fashion enable the ceremony to speak more immediately, and hence effectively, to the witnessing audience?

Orthodoxy, by its nature, is resistant to the very notion of religion-in-the-making. To be worthy, religion must be revealed to humans, directly or indirectly, by God. Of course there are many customs and ceremonies in traditional Judaism, including the naming of daughters, which are the creations of the rabbis of the Talmud and the medieval sages. But the rabbinic tradition creates only where there is divine mandate to do so. There can never legitimately be in Judaism women rabbis, mothers joining fathers on the *bimah*, or kisses and hugs from the rabbi. These are beyond the limits of divine sanction. They are the mere inventions of humans to keep in step with contemporary culture.

Human invention in religion is not considered to be a negative process at Temple Akiba. Judaism is viewed as a historically developing religion, and that development continues to this day. Were baby Jessica's mother not the niece of two rabbis, but the non-Jewish partner in an interfaith marriage, this naming ceremony could have proceeded as long as both parents agreed to raise Jessica as a Jew. That permission, granted only in the last decade, distinguishes Reform Judaism from Conservative and Orthodox Judaism, which would not permit the naming without the mother's prior conversion.

Does it make a difference that even though the Orthodox community does all it can to minimize the role of invention in religion, the liberal community proudly concedes the role of invention? Does it matter that everyone knows that women rabbis are a recent phenomenon? Does it matter that before the 1983 patrilineal descent decision by the Reform movement, the daughter of a non-Jewish mother would not have been named in a temple? Does it matter that even today this child would not be recognized in much of the Jewish community and in Israel as a Jew? And if it does matter, to whom and with what effect?

One way of viewing religion-in-the-making is to say that the validity of this naming ceremony arises not from its longstanding place in Jewish history or its origin in divine revelation, but primarily from this community's acceptance of this ceremony as reflective of its value system. As long as that communal acceptance is clear and undisputed, it makes sense to give Jessica the Hebrew name of *Sh'lomit* and expect that she will grow up as a member in good standing of the contemporary American Reform Jewish community. But inasmuch as this community does not live an isolated existence, and its members interact frequently with the world around them, there remains the lingering question of a broader validation. There remains an ongoing tension between fashioning those religious ceremonies that reflect the values of this community and giving its members legitimated entrée into the larger, world Jewish community.[12]

Dream World or Meaningful Culture?

Barbara Myerhoff reports the following conversation between herself and her "philosopher" informant Shmuel about a graduation *siyum* that took place at the Center and celebrated some of the elderly members' completion of a course of Jewish study. First the skeptical voice of Shmuel:

> This gives them more encouragement for their foolishness. What I object to is how they refuse to accept reality. They think they can make it themselves. . . . They live in a dream world.

For Shmuel, the Eastern European Jew, Judaism is a reality that one accepts or rejects, but that cannot be altered at will. A *siyum* is for completing the study of a tractate of Talmud, not a course on Judaica at a center for the elderly. To call their ceremony a *siyum* is to mix up categories, to tell a story which is not true, to live in a dream world. I hear Shmuel's Eastern European accented words clearly as I write about Jessica's baby naming. Do the rabbis at Temple Akiba live in a dream world where they think they can make up the rules of Judaism as they wish? Is there not a historical and theological reality to Judaism that cannot be so readily altered? Is their community's acceptance a sufficient warrant to welcome the daughter of an interfaith family into the Jewish people?

Here is Myerhoff's response to Shmuel:

> "All right, Shmuel," I replied. "I agree with you, they make things up. But that's what culture is, a set of agreements on how to see the world, how to live and why. They have courage and imagination. . . . I am not as much interested in exaggeration as how they intensify and give significance to ordinary experience. (pp. 110–111)

For Myerhoff, the anthropologist, the fact that these elderly Jews have created out of their Jewish backgrounds a Judaism with which they can live, a Judaism which brings them comfort and meaning, is itself miraculous. That their Judaism is invented is besides the point. All culture is humanly constructed. Even Orthodoxy, from an anthropological perspective, is a human construction.

Judged by Myerhoff's criteria, the Temple Akiba clergy and educators know very well how to "intensify and give significance to ordinary experience." They do this with extraordinary grace. I remember one woman telling of how she received a call from Rabbi Davidman on *erev* (the eve of) Yom Kippur. He called to tell her that he would have her brother, an AIDS patient, in mind during his prayers. She concluded, "Can you believe he would have the time to call me then?"

Hearing this, I thought, this congregant's story is like a present-day version of the famous Hasidic tale of the rebbe disappearing before *Kol Nidre* services to bring kindling wood to the sick widow. Can there be anything more genuinely Jewish than this act of *ḥesed*? Is this not a living Judaism? Does not this Jewish community function to "give significance and meaning" to the lives of its involved members?

But no one incident, no matter how moving, can answer the underlying question. Temple Akiba is undertaking a risky venture in the name of American Judaism.

American Jews have decided to lead their lives in ways that radically depart from the precepts of traditional Judaism. Intermarriage is only the most obvious example. Temple Akiba, like most American synagogues, is inventing a Judaism to speak to contemporary American Jews in ways that connect with their current experience. Will this Judaism prove viable? Will it speak effectively? Will it be a recognizable Judaism to the rest of world Jewry? All these questions remain open.

From an educational perspective, these are the most crucial questions. Synagogue education is itself a wild gamble: that children from diverse families who come for several hours a week to study Hebrew and learn about Judaism will take these matters to heart. We know from every conceivable study that those hours alone will not do the trick. To make a significant difference in their Jewish lives, the children and their families will have to be drawn in more deeply to Jewish life than is possible in those few hours.

I have focused on social drama and ritual as cultural performance for I believe that collective self-definition is a key to synagogue education. If Temple Akiba, or any of its sister congregations, hopes to educate the next generation to live as Jews in America, they will have to define a Judaism that is both identifiable and meaningful. Congregants—young and old—have to know what this Judaism is so that they might embrace it as their own. Has it distinctive features? Do these features make a difference in their lives? Will belonging enhance their lives?

The rabbis and educators at Temple Akiba have risen to the challenge of giving definition to their Judaism. They are not afraid to say, "In this we believe and in this we don't." They are willing to put forward Jewish traditions without assuming them to be binding. They are open to many configurations of the Jewish family without brushing aside the problematic issues involved. They will stand up for a more intensive Jewish education than was offered previously even against the calls for less. They will use all the means available to them to announce who they are and what they stand for, even when doing so creates conflict and sets off social drama.

By working hard at defining a collective identity for this congregation, the rabbis have built upon the long history of this congregation and fashioned a Jewish message that is both clear and controversial. This message is a Reform Judaism with teeth. Uncles Sam and Maurice may each reject this Jewish message for his own reasons. But there is a clear message to be accepted or rejected.

Perhaps this clear sense of collective identity helps explain why I rarely encountered bored children or adults in the many educational contexts of this congregation that I observed. When there is a clear message that gives shape to the educational agenda, children and adults sense that message and respond to it. They are challenged. One can accept or reject it, but it is not so amorphous that it leaves one swimming in confusion or boredom.[13]

As a participant in Temple Akiba, I too experienced the challenge of their collective identity. This was an exciting context within which to do fieldwork. Their Judaism was not one I had previously known, but my informants took every opportunity to educate me about their worldview. Finally, I too was one of their students, and I have tried to testify to the skill of their educational approach.

The most significant question is the one I cannot answer: Will this Judaism, this religion-in-the-making, prove convincing and moving to their members? Will the children and adults whom I observed take this Judaism to heart and make it a living part of their lives? That, after all, is the ultimate educational question. But ethnographies cannot answer ultimate questions. Until the record is more complete, answering that question will remain a matter of faith.

Notes

Chapter 1: The Educating Synagogue

1. Mordechai M. Kaplan, *Judaism as a Civilization: Toward a Reconstruction of American-Jewish Life* (New York: Schocken Books, 1967 [originally 1934]).
2. For a cross-cultural perspective on Jewish education, see H.S. Himmelfarb and S. DellaPergola, eds., *Jewish Education Worldwide: Cross-Cultural Perspectives* (Lanham, Md.: University Press of America, 1989). For the unique role of the American synagogue, see Barry Chazan, "Education in the Synagogue: The Transformation of the Supplementary School" in Jack Wertheimer, ed., *The American Synagogue: A Sanctuary Transformed* (New York: Cambridge University Press, 1987).
3. Scholarly reviews include: Harold S. Himmelfarb, "The Non-Linear Impact of Schooling: Comparing Different Types and Amounts of Jewish Education," *Sociology of Education* 42 (April 1977): 114–29; Geoffrey S. Bock, "Does Jewish Education Matter?" *Jewish Education and Jewish Identity* (New York: American Jewish Committee, 1977); Board of Jewish Education of Greater New York, *Jewish Supplementary Schooling: An Educational System in Need of Change* (New York: Board of Jewish Education, 1988); David Schoem, *Ethnic Survival In America: An Ethnography of a Jewish Afternoon School* (Atlanta: Scholars Press, 1989).
4. Jack Wertheimer, *A People Divided: Judaism in Contemporary America* (New York: Basic Books, 1993): 43–65.
5. Steven M. Cohen, *American Assimilation or Jewish Renewal* (Bloomington, Ind.: Indiana University Press, 1988). Cohen was the first social scientist to suggest that attending synagogue schools could have a positive relation to adult Jewish commitment.
6. Gary A. Tobin and Gabriel Berger, *Synagogue Affiliation: Implications for the 1990's,* Research Report 9 (Waltham, Mass: Cohen Center for Modern Jewish Studies, 1993): 13.
7. An outstanding example of this focus is evident in *Jewish Supplementary Schooling: An Educational System in Need of Change* cited in note 3 above.
8. Schoem, op. cit., 29.
9. Wertheimer, 49–51. Also see Sidney Goldstein, "Profile of American Jewry: Insights from the National Jewish Population Survey," *American Jewish Yearbook* (New York: American Jewish Committee, 1992): 77–173.

10. Synagogue affiliation is affected by a number of variables including age, income, education, and geographic region. Yet, Tobin and Berger (1993) conclude: "Having children enrolled in formal Jewish education maintains its character as the strongest predictor of synagogue affiliation" (p. 23).
11. Isa Aron, "The Malaise of Jewish Education," *Tikkun* 4 (1989): 32–34.
12. See Hope Jensen Leichter, ed., *The Family as Educator* (New York: Teachers College Press, 1977) for a powerful set of arguments on how families educate their own members and modify the educational messages of the school system. Leichter's work does not refer to religious education, but I believe that the same case can be made for the family in relation to the synagogue.
13. Philip Roth, *Goodbye, Columbus and Five Short Stories* (Boston: Houghton Mifflin, 1989): 137–58.
14. See especially Schoem's nonfictional, ethnographic description of the Hebrew school classrooms in *Ethnic Survival in America*, Chapter 7.
15. See J. Snarey, J. Reimer, and L. Kohlberg, "The Kibbutz as Model for Moral Education: A Longitudinal Study," *Journal of Applied Developmental Psychology* 6 (1985). Also, Joseph Reimer, "Moral Education: The Just Community Approach," *Phi Delta Kappan* 62 (1981).
16. For a powerful discussion of this balance, see Victor Turner's forward to Barbara Myerhoff, *Number Our Days* (New York: E. P. Dutton, 1979). Also, David M. Fetterman, *Ethnography Step by Step* (Newbury Park, Calif.: Sage Publications, 1989): 32–34.
17. Among the ten leaders interviewed were two congregational rabbis (Conservative and Reform), two executives of denominational offices (Conservative and Reform), a high-ranking staff member from the local federation and the local bureau, the executive from the local synagogue council, a day-school principal, a synagogue administrator, and a leading lay leader active in both federation and synagogue circles.
18. Four of these professionals were principals of local synagogue schools (two from each of the denominations, Conservative and Reform), three were from the local Bureau of Jewish Education, which has supervisory responsibilities for these schools, and one was from the local federation and served as a liaison to the educational community.
19. Within this Jewish community there are also Orthodox synagogues as well as Reconstructionist and independent *minyanim* (informal prayer groups). But the Orthodox community—with only one exception—rely on day-school education and no longer maintain synagogue schools. Some of the independent groups do maintain schools, but they are not the focus of this study.
20. Of the ten schools cited, six were Reform and four were Conservative. I asked what accounts for the goodness of these programs, and respondents cited these factors (in order of frequency

mentioned): the school director, the support of the community, the vision of the rabbi, the quality of the teachers, the degree of parental involvement, and the thoughtfulness of the curriculum.

21. All names associated with the research are pseudonyms, including the names of synagogues, rabbis, educators, parents, and children.

22. On informants in ethnographic research, see Pertti J. Pelto, *Anthropological Research: The Structure of Inquiry.* (New York: Harper and Row, 1970): 95–98.

23. This portrait would be written for the Commission on Jewish Education in North America for which I worked as a staff member. This phase of the research was supported by the Mandel Associated Foundations of Cleveland, Ohio. I used Sara Lawrence Lightfoot's concept of a school portrait as a model for this work. See *The Good High School: Portraits of Character and Culture* (New York: Basic Books, 1983).

24. These numbers—and all similar descriptors of the synagogues—are from 1990 when the study was under way.

25. Joseph Reimer, *The Synagogue as a Context for Jewish Education* (Cleveland: Commission of Jewish Education in North America, 1990).

26. Of the ethnographies of American synagogue life, I cite a few which have influenced this work:
Frieda Kerner Furman, *Beyond Yiddishkeit: The Struggle for Jewish Identity in a Reform Synagogue* (Buffalo, N.Y.: State University of New York Press, 1987).
Samuel C. Heilman, *Synagogue Life: A Study in Symbolic Interaction* (Chicago: University of Chicago Press, 1976).
Jack Kugelmass, *The Miracle of Intervale Avenue: The Story of a Jewish Congregation in the South Bronx* (New York: Schocken, 1986).
Riv-Ellen Prell, *Prayer and Community: The Havurah in American Judaism* (Detroit: Wayne State University Press, 1989).

27. Barbara Myerhoff, *Number our Days* (New York: Dutton, 1979). op. cit.

28. I develop this view at greater length in chapter 6.

29. See Victor Turner, *Dramas, Fields, and Metaphors: Symbolic Action in Human Society* (Ithaca, N.Y.: Cornell University Press, 1974).

30. Although he would make this point using a different set of analytic tools, see Edwin H. Friedman, *Generation to Generation: Family Process in Church and Synagogue* (New York: Guilford Press, 1985) for powerful illustrations of drama in synagogue life.

31. Samuel C. Heilman, *The People of the Book: Drama, Fellowship and Religion* (Chicago: University of Chicago Press, 1983): 25.

Chapter 2: Educating the Adults

1. See Heilman's description of six different approaches within the Orthodox community to Torah study in Samuel C. Heilman, *The People of the Book: Drama, Fellowship, and Religion* (Chicago: University of Chicago Press, 1983): 8–24.

2. Barry W. Holtz in his chapter on midrash describes this literature as follows: "To begin with we should make clear that there is no single book called the midrash. Midrash is a type of literature . . . a kind of process or activity, but there is no one midrash. Rather there are collections of midrashim (pl.) which were put together at various times and by various editors over the course of many hundreds of years. The great flowering of midrash was roughly between 400 and 1200 C.E. . . . But it is important to note that originally, midrashic literature was oral—sermons preached in the synagogues and teachings of various sages. . . . What, then, is midrash? It is helpful to think of midrash in two different, but related ways: first, midrash (deriving from the Hebrew root "to search out") is the process of interpreting. The object of interpretation is the Bible or, on occasion, other sacred texts; second, midrash refers to the corpus of work that has collected these interpretations, works such as Midrash Rabbah." The *Encyclopedia Judaica* dates Exodus Rabbah in the period of 900–1000 C.E., which is well after the editing of the Babylonian Talmud, but still earlier than the editing of the late anthologies of midrash. See this cited in Barry Holtz, *Back to the Sources* (New York: Summit Books, 1984): 177–180.

3. Rabbi Davidman specifically referred to the *Mekhilta,* a midrash on Exodus written in that early, Tannaitic Period before 200 C.E. See *Back to the Sources,* 188.

4. He refers to a famous letter that Maimonides, the outstanding medieval Jewish scholar (11351–1204), wrote to a proselyte named Obadia. See: Isadore Twersky, *A Maimonides Reader* (New York: Behrman House, 1972): 474–76. Twersky comments about this letter that "Maimonides encourages [Obadia] by expounding a lofty, spiritual conception of Judaism in which biological factors are rather insignificant" (p. 474).

5. For the origins of Hebrew Union College, see Marc Lee Raphael, *Profiles in American Judaism* (San Francisco: Harper and Row, 1984): 16–19.

6. For an early embrace by American Reform Movement of modern biblical criticism, see Michael A. Meyer, *Response to Modernity: A History of the Reform Movement in Judaism* (New York: Oxford University Press, 1988): 272–74.

7. On the continuing tension between the study of rabbinic literature and of biblical criticism in rabbinical school curriculum, see Charles S. Liebman, *Aspects of the Religious Behavior of American Jews* (New York: Ktav Publishing, 1974): 97. I do not mean to suggest that rabbis found it easy to translate scholarship into sermons.

8. For a clear articulation of the faith of "Prophetism" in contrast to "yoke of Mosaic–Talmudic Judaism" see Kaufman Kohler's "Backward or Forwards?" as quoted in Sylvan D. Schwartzman, *Reform Judaism Then and Now* (New York: UAHC, 1971): 220–21. There have been many adjustments in Reform Jewish thought on this issue. For more recent rethinking, see Eugene B. Borowitz, *Reform Judaism Today* (New York: Behrman House, 1978), especially the chapter on "The Lessons Reform Judaism has Learned."

9. See Meyer, pp. 373–78, for growing trend in contemporary Reform Movement towards traditionalism. See also, Marc Lee Raphael, *Profiles in American Judaism*, 58–62.

10. Barbara Myerhoff, *Number our Days*, p. 221.

11. See Meyer, pp. 272–76, on early twentieth-century radical Reform as embodied by Emil G. Hirsch. See pp. 326–34 for the practice of Sunday services in early 20th century Reform congregations.

12. See Meyer, pp. 272–76, for a definition and description of classical Reform as embodied by Kaufman Kohler.

13. See Meyer, pp. 326–34, and Raphael, pp. 40–43, for "the explosive issue of Zionism" in the Reform of the 1930s.

14. My observations stand in contrast to what Furman (1987) reports in her participant observation study of "Temple Shalom," a Reform Synagogue on the West Coast. She writes: "At Temple Shalom the absence of a wholehearted commitment to any one element of the tradition, religious, nationalistic, ethnic or cultural, results in an ambiguous sense of Jewish identity. Secondly, the universalistic and modernist commitments of the members of Temple Shalom a priori set themselves against an appreciation of ancient and frequently particularistic tradition" (p. 57). The difference highlights the individual characters of the congregations and even regions of the country, although the difference of several years between studies could also be a factor. See Frieda Kerner Furman, *Beyond Yiddishkeit: The Struggle for Jewish Identity in a Reform Synagogue* (Albany: State University of New York Press, 1987).

15. See Leon Jick, *The Americanization of the Synagogue, 1820–1870* (Hanover, N.H.: Brandeis University Press, 1976), for the early changes in worship. See Meyer, pp. 320–22, for changes in the 1920s and 1930s, and pp. 373–77, for changes in the 1960s and 1970s. See Raphael, pp. 64–68, on more recent changes in worship.

16. By "modify," I mean that I had no original plan to collaborate in planning a service. But my experience in my fieldwork on a kibbutz taught me that working with informants can bring you closer and gain you greater insider status. I found that was the case in Temple Akiba. I seemed to be more accepted by the clergy team after this point.

17. The first woman to be ordained as a rabbi from Hebrew Union College–Jewish Institute of Religion was Sally Preisand in 1972 (Meyer, p. 379). The numbers have increased since then, with

Raphael reporting (p. 69) that by "the early 1980's more than 75 women had been ordained." Yet a woman rabbi on the pulpit is still a novelty in certain congregations.

18. For more background on Jewish family education, see Joseph Reimer, "Family Education" in *What We Know About Jewish Education*, S. L. Kelman, ed. (Los Angeles: Torah Aura Productions, 1992).

19. An excellent source on *shivah* and the other traditional Jewish customs of mourning is Maurice Lamm, *The Jewish Way in Death and Mourning* (New York: Jonathan David Publishers, 1969). On *shivah*, see pp. 77ff.

20. See Myerhoff, pp. 32–33, 185–87.

Chapter 3: The Temple Akiba School

1. The Hebrew program of the school will be described fully later in this chapter and in Chapter 5.

2. "*Halakhah*" is the Hebrew term for the Jewish legal process. The Reform movement began as an effort to reform the *halakhah* to find "more adequate means to give expression to the spirit of Judaism and to reveal its character of universal religion." While the movement has contintually "asserted the right of individual self-determination" in matters of religious observance, in recent years "Reform Jews have taken greater interest in having ritual guidance" and some rabbis have been "proponents of a Reform *halakhah*." Yet Reform *halakhah*—in distinction to the more traditional *halakhah*—is not binding, but represents "resources to utilize in full personal freedom." Eugene Borowitz, *Liberal Judaism*. New York: UAHC, 1984, pp. 327–330.

3. For a fuller description of the Reform position on the issue of patrilineal descent, see Walter Jacob, *Contemporary American Reform Response*. New York: Central Conference of American Rabbis, 1987, pp. 61–69.

4. To investigate *diversity* as a more observable phenomenon, I began looking at classroom rosters to check for last names. As an example, in one Hebrew class I found some typical Jewish names, such as Cohen, Levy, and Rosenberg. But I also found some names, such as Kelly, Gallico, and Adams, associated with other ethnic groups. There was quite a mix.

5. This was the issue of controversy in the family education session in Chapter 2. In addition to the nontraditional American families, there are close to thirty children in the school from newly arrived Russian families, making the mix even richer.

6. Janet Aviad, *Return to Judaism* (Chicago: University of Chicago Press, 1983).

7. Schoem offers illustrations from the school that he studied of maximizing strategies. See Chapters 6–8.

8. See Schoem, p. 96. Also see Samuel C. Heilman, *Inside the Jewish School: A Study of the Cultural Setting for Jewish Education* (New York: American Jewish Committee, Institute of Human Relations, 1985): 11.

9. During the second year of the study, the 1990 National Jewish Population Survey was released in preliminary form and caused a great stir in documenting an accelerated pace of Jewish assimilation into American culture. See, *Highlights of CJF 1990 National Jewish Population Survey* (New York: Council of Jewish Federations, 1991).

10. Rabbi Davidman has taken a strong position on welcoming the membership of the *ger toshav*, the non-Jew who has chosen to join the synagogue and supports the raising of his or her children as Jews. His welcoming stance—which I am calling "minimalist"—is not universally shared by his rabbinic colleagues in the Reform movement.

11. In an interview I conducted at the beginning of this study, a prominent Conservative rabbi made clear his disapproval of congregational rabbis moving into the educational role. "If a person has invested five years of studying for the rabbinate, why take a job as educator which you can get without that training?" He thought it important "to highlight the special calling of the rabbinate." While he was not referring to Don Marcus, I think this is a common view of rabbis' relations to Jewish education. I am arguing by presenting the case of Don Marcus that this view may need to be reconsidered.

12. By the mid-1990s, Don had left Temple Akiba to become the senior rabbi of a synagogue in another metropolitan area.

13. At the one board meeting I was invited to attend, the major issue of discussion was the substantial number of members who—in a recessionary economy—were very late in paying their dues. A proposal was made that if bills were not paid by a certain date, those members would lose their rights to use synagogue services. The regular service that is used by many is children's attendance in the school. Don protested: "Let's not use the children as pawns. Treat them as everyone else." He was joined by some laypeople who shared his concern. A compromise position was agreed upon that they would issue a warning, but be less immediately punitive to parents.

14. These figures are for the religious school, grades K–8. They do not include the high school. In comparing the Temple Akiba enrollments to parallel schools in the immediate area, Don is referring to two large synagogues—one Conservative and one Reform—that have lost enrollment in the years that this school has grown. In the larger metropolitan area, Temple Akiba is one of six synagogues with schools that have enrollments of more than three hundred children.

15. The educational budget of the temple covers more functions than the school alone. It also covers the salaries of the youth advisor and librarian and items for informal education such as youth groups and *kallot* (retreats).

16. Temple Akiba has the policy of not charging tuition for the school above the cost of membership. Most synagogues, like Temple Hillel,

subsidize the cost of the school, but still charge some tuition beyond membership. The rationale for this policy, as presented in the temple literature, is: "We believe so strongly in education as the foundation of understanding that for Temple members there is no additional cost for [educational programs]." That is true for tuition, but there are fees for certain activities and the cost of the tutorial program.

17. The number of students in grades 9–12 has increased in each of the past four years from thirty-four to sixty-two students. In terms of retention, if we look at the current ninth and current tenth grades over the past years, we find:

	(1) Ninth-graders	(2) Tenth-graders
7th grade	43 students	50 students
8th grade	42 students	38 students
9th grade	28 students	23 students
10th grade	———	15 students

A great majority of both classes continued to eighth grade, and in one class 65 percent of the original group continued to ninth grade, although in the second only 46 percent continued. Every class shows some percentage of drop-off from year to year, but the patterns are quite different for these two cohorts.

18. For a description of seriously disruptive behavioral problems in a synagogue school, see Schoem, pp. 101–11.

19. Jonathan Woocher, *Sacred Survival: The Civil Religion of American Jews* (Bloomington: Indiana University Press, 1986). The Israel fair, which attracted a throng of parents and children, featured Israeli foods, artifacts, and small farm animals. It had a carnival atmosphere and was a fun event for participants. It had no direct relation to the synagogue as "religious" center, but was a clear reflection of the synagogue and school's providing opportunities for celebrating the "civil religion"— that is, Jews' attachment to Israel and its culture.

20. *Classical Hebrew* is an umbrella term that refers to the Hebrew of the Bible, the rabbinic, and medieval periods. In sum, the Hebrew of sacred purposes such as prayer and study. *Modern Hebrew* refers to the rebirth of Hebrew as a modern language in the nineteenth and twentieth centuries. This Hebrew has evolved into the official spoken language of the State of Israel. For a fuller treatment, see Shalom Spiegel, *Hebrew Reborn* (New York: Meridien Books, 1962).

21. Looking at the educational budget shows how heavy an investment is made in the Hebrew program. The total figure for salaries of religious school teachers is $60,000, while for Hebrew teachers it is $78,000. The average salary for religious school teachers is $2,700; for Hebrew teachers it is $5,400. Hebrew teachers teach more hours and are on the average more experienced than other teachers and hence are paid more. But it is the religious school teachers who teach the larger number of students.

Chapter 4: A Close Look at Classroom Learning

1. Bible stories are first introduced as part of the second-grade curriculum, using D. Meilach's *First Book of Bible Heroes* (Ktav, 1963). During third grade, S. Rossel's *A Child's Bible: Lessons from the Torah* (Behrman House, 1988) is introduced and its second volume is also used in fourth grade. In fifth grade Simon and Bial's *The Rabbi's Bible* (Behrman House, 1969) is introduced. The emphasis in sixth grade shifts to Jewish lifecycle and Jewish history. In seventh and eighth grades the students use *The Torah* (Jewish Publication Society) as their text.

2. See Samuel C. Heilman, *The People of the Book: Drama, Fellowship, and Religion* and *Inside the Jewish School*, op. cit.

3. Jean Piaget, *Six Psychological Studies* (New York: Vintage Books, 1967).

4. S. Heilman, *Inside the Jewish School*, p. 8.

5. At the suggestion of the veteran sixth-grade Hebrew teacher, this group was selected in sixth grade to study with her at an accelerated pace. For the first time a homogeneous grouping was allowed. Both Don and Ann, the Hebrew coordinator, considered this decision to be a mistake since it also created a much weaker second class of Hebrew students who, in my observation, were the only Hebrew class to exhibit regular behavioral problems. You could often hear noise emanating from their room, and in fact, their teacher was let go in midyear. The new teacher brought a much improved situation, but the divergence in Hebrew levels persisted.

6. The students are reading the Hebrew text, but I am providing an English translation for the Hebrew from *Tanakh* (Philadelphia: Jewish Publication Society, 1985): 1037. The students do not have this translation available in class and are themselves translating from the Hebrew.

7. See, for example, the scholarly commentary on Jonah in *Five Megillot* (Philadelphia: Jewish Publication Society, 1970).

8. Heilman is adopting the terms "flood out" and "out of play" from Erving Goffman's work. See *Encounters* (Indianapolis: Bobbs-Merrill, 1961): 55–57 and *Frame Analysis* (Cambridge: Harvard University Press, 1974): 346.

9. R. J .Z. Werblowsky and G. Wigoder, eds., *The Encyclopedia of the Jewish Religion* (New York: Holt, Rinehart, and Winston, 1965): p. 101.

Chapter 5: The "Mandatory Hebrew" Controversy

1. My use of "culture of the congregation" is influenced by Seymour B. Sarason's *The Culture of the School and the Problem of Change* (Boston: Allyn and Bacon, 1971), Barbara Myerhoff's *Number Our Days* (New York: E. F. Dutton, 1979) on the culture of a senior adult center, David Schoem's *Ethnic Survival in America: An Ethnography of a Jewish Afternoon School* (Atlanta: Scholars Press, 1989), and Susan Shevitz's "An Organizational Perspective on Changing Congregational Education: What the Literature Reveals" (in *A Congregation of Learners*. Eds. Isa Aron, Sara Lee, Seymour Rossel. New York: UAHC Press, 1995). I am contending that over time synagogues, as religious organizations, develop a view of the world and their place in that world that sets standards of appropriate thought and behavior for that synagogue. Denominational affiliation plays but a part in establishing that culture. In moving from congregation to congregation, one can sense that for all the commonality, each is a world unto itself. My larger claim is that to understand how Jewish education functions within a synagogue, one first has to understand the culture of that congregation, for it is that culture that sets the parameters for the decision about education.

2. For a more detailed description of the philosophy of the Melton Hebrew Program, see Ruth Raphaeli, "The Melton Curriculum and the Melton Hebrew Language Program for Afternoon Hebrew Schools," in *Studies in Jewish Education*, vol. 4 (Jerusalem: Hebrew University Press, 1989).

3. For more detailed descriptions of classroom observations in the Hebrew program, see Joseph Reimer, "Temple Akiba," in Council for Initiatives in Jewish Education, *Best Practices Project: The Supplementary School* (1993): 95–111.

4. This account of the RSC's handling of the issue of mandatory Hebrew over this two-year span was provided by Sherry Saunders, the chair, in an April interview.

5. Don Marcus reported that the RSC's process of reviewing the school curriculum and the place of Hebrew in it began back in 1985–86. It took several years for the RSC to reach a point of knowledge and confidence to consider the "mandatory Hebrew" proposal.

6. These statements are quoted from the "Report to the Board of Trustees of a Change in Policy Regarding the Study of Hebrew" that Sherry Saunders wrote in December on behalf of the RSC.

7. Barbara, Myerhoff, *Number Our Days*, N.Y., E. F. Dutton, 1979, pp. 142–48, makes a convincing argument that people without much political power in an organization will stage a protest more in the hope of gaining visibility and presence than of changing organizational policy. I think that that dynamic may be operative here. I am

calling that a "ritual" protest.

8. *Highlights of the 1990 National Jewish Population Survey* (New York: Council of Jewish Federations, 1991).

Chapter 6: Synagogue Drama and Education

1. For models of exploring other educating synagogues, see I. Aron, S. Lee, and S. Rossel, eds., *A Congregation of Learners: Transforming the Synagogue into a Learning Community* (New York: UAHC Press, 1995).

2. Jack Wertheimer, *A People Divided: Judaism in Contemporary America* (New York: Basic Books, 1993).

3. The heart of Wertheimer's case is presented in Part III of *A People Divided*, "The Fragmenting World of Organized Judaism," pp. 95–184.

4. When the Lubavitcher Rebbe died, the story was given front-page coverage in the *New York Times*, June 13, 1994. By then, of course, the Lubavitcher had become a regular feature of metropolitan coverage for the *Times*, including a cover story in the *Sunday Magazine*, March 15, 1992.

5. For an insightful treatment of the nonrational features of synagogue organization, see, Susan L. Shevitz, "An Organizational Perspective on Changing Congregational Education." In, *Congregation of Learners* (1995): 155–84.

6. In recent years the Reform movement has grown in numbers and replaced the Conservative movement as the denomination with which the most American Jews identify. Yet, in terms of actual synagogue affiliation, the Conservative movement still has the higher percentages than Reform. See, Wertheimer, *A People Divided*, pp. 52–53.

7. Even in the Orthodox context Heilman notes the phenomenon of rebellion against the rabbi as part of the dynamics of a social drama. See, Heilman, *People of the Book*, pp. 39–43.

8. Roth captures just that possibility taken to comic extremes in his story "The Conversion of the Jews."

9. Heilman beautifully captures the tension of the liminal movement, but also the pressure from within the learning group towards resolution and the redressive steps taken by key actors in the drama in "The case of the puzzling redundancy." See *The People of the Book*, pp. 31–48.

10. I try to illustrate these points in my article abut a social drama at Temple Hillel. See Joseph Reimer, "Between Parents and Principal: Social Drama in a Synagogue School," *Contemporary Jewry*, 13 (1993): 60–73.

11. This *sukkah* on the *bimah* is a symbolic reminder, but not a replacement of the outdoor *sukkah*.

12. This tension was reflected in my interview with Rabbi Davidman. In

talking about the process of conversion, Norman said he presses the convert to undergo conversion in a more traditional manner—e.g., use of the ritual bath—than is required by Reform practice. This is to help assure acceptance of the conversion at least in Conservative circles, and hence give the Jew-by-choice a broader Jewish community in which to live a Jewish life.

13. For the contrasting condition, see David Schoem's *Ethnic Survival in America: An Ethnography of a Jewish Afternoon School* (Atlanta: Scholars Press, 1989). It shows the educational results of there not being a clear sense of collective identity in a congregation. In this case, neither teachers nor students have a clear sense of why they are there or what they are supposed to be learning. Confusion reigns.

Glossary

aliyah — Literally, "going up." In synagogue it commonly refers to going up to the *bimah* (see below) to recite the blessings over the reading of the Torah scroll.

bimah — Raised pulpit often at the front of the sanctuary from which prayer services are led.

Classical Reform Judaism — Refers to the formative period in the development of Reform Judaism in North America (1880–1920) and to a set of core beliefs about Judaism that continue to exert influence in Temple Akiba and other Reform congregations.

erev — Literally, "evening." Often refers to the evening (or, by extension, the day) before a Jewish holiday.

haggadah — The liturgical book that is recited at the Passover seder.

halakhah — Literally, "the way." The corpus of Jewish law. *Halakhic* often refers to a traditional—many times Orthodox—way of interpreting Jewish law. But the Conservative and Reform movements also refer to their halakhah.

havdalah — The Saturday night ritual—using a candle, wine and spices—that separates the holiness of the Sabbath from the other days of the week.

ḥesed — An act of loving kindness.

Jew-by-choice — The term favored by many to refer to a person who has chosen to become a Jew through conversion.

kallah — Literally, a bride. By extension, a retreat on the Sabbath. Often refers to a Sabbath event for teens.

kippah — Traditional head cover (skullcap) worn in synagogue or at home for religious activity. Traditionally worn by men; recently also by some women.

midrash — A type of rabbinic literature that interprets the Bible. Also refers to the corpus of literature that was collected over many hundreds of years.

mitzvah (plural: mitzvot) — A religious obligation. Sometimes used as a synonym for a righteous act.

posek — A rabbinic authority with the power to adjudicate halakhic questions for a given community.

Kabbalat Shabbat — Traditional Friday evening prayer service that welcomes in the Sabbath (Shabbat).

refusniks — Jews in the former Soviet Union whose requests for exit visas were refused by the Soviet authorities. In many cases they lost their jobs and were ostracized by Soviet society.

Seliḥot — Penitential prayers traditionally recited the Saturday night before Rosh Hashanah to prepare the congregation to enter the solemn mood of the High Holidays.

shivah — Literally, sitting. The traditional seven-day period of mourning after a funeral in which the official mourners "sit" at home and receive comfort from visitors who pay a *shivah* call.

Sh'ma — The central Jewish prayer, "Hear O Israel," recited at both the morning and evening services.

Simḥat Torah — Rejoicing over the Torah. A holiday during which Jews in synagogues dance with the Torah to celebrate the completion of a year's cycle of Torah reading.

siyum — Traditionally a celebration to mark the completion of a volume of Jewish study, often talmudic study (see below).

sukkah — A booth erected for the holiday of Sukkot that commemorates the Jews wondering in the Sinai desert after the exodus from Egypt.

tallit — A prayer shawl worn during services. Traditionally worn by men. Recently worn by some women.

Talmud — The codified oral law together with rabbinic commentaries.

tsimmes — A traditional Eastern European sweet stew made of available vegetables and fruits.

tzedakah — Literally, an act of justice. Often refers to the giving of charity.

yeshivah — An academy for advanced talmudic learning, traditionally open only to Orthodox male students.

Yiddishkeit — *Jewishness* in Yiddish. The lived, domestic religious culture of Eastern European Jews.

Selected Bibliography

Aron, Isa. "The Malaise of Jewish Education." *Tikkun* 4 (1989): 32–34.

Aron, I., Lee and S. Rossel, eds. *A Congregation of Learners: Transforming the Synagogue into a Learning Community*. New York: UAHC Press, 1995.

Board of Jewish Education of Greater New York. *Jewish Supplementary Schooling: An Educational System in Need of Change*. New York: Board of Jewish Education, 1988.

Cohen, Steven M. *American Assimilation or Jewish Renewal?* Bloomington, Ind.: Indiana University Press, 1988.

Furman, Frieda Kerner. *Beyond Yiddishkeit: The Struggle for Jewish Identity in a Reform Synagogue*. Albany, New York: State University of New York Press, 1987.

Heilman, Samuel C. *The People of the Book: Drama, Fellowship, and Religion*. Chicago: University of Chicago Press, 1983.

———— *Inside the Jewish School: A Study of the Cultural Setting for Jewish Education*. New York: American Jewish Committee, Institute of Human Relations, 1985.

Kosmin, Barry A., et. al. *Highlights of the National Jewish Population Survey*. New York: Council of Jewish Federations, 1991.

Meyer, Michael A. *Response to Modernity: A History of the Reform Movement in Judaism*. New York: Oxford University Press, 1988.

Myerhoff, Barbara. *Number Our Days*. New York: E. P. Dutton, 1979.

Raphael, Marc Lee. *Profiles in American Judaism*. San Francisco: Harper and Row, 1984.

Reimer, Joseph. *The Synagogue as a Context for Jewish Education*. Cleveland: Commission on Jewish Education in North America, 1990.

———— "Between Parents and Principal: Social Drama in a Synagogue School." *Contemporary Jewry* 13 (1993): 60–73.

Roth, Philip. "The Conversion of the Jews." In *Goodbye, Columbus and Five Short Stories*. Boston: Houghton Mifflin, 1989.

Schoem, David. *Ethnic Survival in America: An Ethnography of a Jewish Afternoon School*. Atlanta: Scholars Press, 1989.

Tobin, Gary A. and Gabriel Berger. *Synagogue Affiliation: Implications for the 1990s*. Research Report 9, Waltham, Mass.: Cohen Center for Modern Jewish Studies, 1993.

Turner, Victor. *Dramas, Fields and Metaphors: Symbolic Actions in Human Society*. Ithaca, N.Y.: Cornell University Press, 1974.

Wertheimer, Jack, ed. *The American Synagogue: A Sanctuary Transformed*. New York: Cambridge University Press, 1987.

————*A People Divided: Judaism in Contemporary America*. New York: Basic Books, 1993.